The Walter Lynwood Fleming Lectures in Southern History

Behind the Lines in the Southern Confederacy

Behind the Lines in the Southern Confederacy

CHARLES W. RAMSDELL

Edited with a Foreword by

WENDELL H. STEPHENSON

Louisiana State University Press

Baton Rouge and London

Copyright © 1944, 1972 by Louisiana State University Press
All rights reserved
Manufactured in the United States of America

Louisiana Paperback Edition, 1997
06 05 04 03 02 01 00 99 98 97   5 4 3 2 1

Library of Congress Cataloging-in-Publication Data

Ramsdell, Charles W. (Charles William), 1877–1942.
    Behind the lines in the Southern Confederacy / by Charles W.
Ramsdell: edited with a foreword by Wendell H. Stephenson.– La.
pbk. ed.
        p. cm.– (Walter Lynwood Fleming lectures in southern
history)
    Includes bibliographical references (p.).
    ISBN 0-8071-2186-X (p : alk.paper)
    1. Confederate States of America–Social conditions.
2. Confederate States of America–Economic conditions.
3. Confederate States of America–Politics and government.
I. Stephenson, Wendell Holmes, 1899–1970. II. Title. III. Series.
E487.R2 1997
973.7' 13–dc21
                                                                96-45592
                                                                     CIP

The paper in this book meets the guidelines for permanence and durability of the Committee on Production Guidelines for Book Longevity of the Council on Library Resources. ♾

FOREWORD

The Walter Lynwood Fleming Lectures in Southern History were inaugurated at Louisiana State University in 1937. They were named in honor of a former professor of history who distinguished himself as a scholar, researcher, and writer in the Reconstruction period. Fleming was a native of the South and a graduate of Alabama Polytechnic Institute and Columbia University. He taught at West Virginia University in his early years and completed his professional career at Vanderbilt University, but the decade he served at Louisiana State University, 1907–1917, was a significant period in the development of a scholarly mind. As a historian his name stands for impartial yet sympathetic investigation of an important epoch of southern history.

It was unusually appropriate that Dr. Charles W. Ramsdell should be chosen to give the inaugural series of lectures. He, like Fleming, received his doctorate at Columbia University under the tutelage of William A. Dunning. Each investigated a segment of the history of his native state as a dissertation: Fleming, *The Civil War and Reconstruction in Alabama;* Ramsdell, *Reconstruction in Texas*. Fleming soon turned to the

Reconstruction epoch as a field of concentration, while Ramsdell established an enviable reputation as an authority on the Southern Confederacy.

Ramsdell chose as the central theme of his lectures, "Behind the Lines in the Southern Confederacy." The series was scheduled for immediate publication by the University Press, but the ever-meticulous scholar desired to give them another revision. That he worked on them from time to time is evidenced by some rephrasing, marginal queries, and footnote indexes. He did not find it possible, however, to give them careful consideration, and repeated pleas by the present writer failed to convince the author that the lectures merited publication without revision. Their excellence would seem to warrant posthumous printing despite a lack of finishing touches which Ramsdell would have given them.

Early drafts as well as the completed manuscript reveal in part the author's method of work. He first prepared a detailed outline. He comprehended his subject so clearly that few departures in organization or subject matter were necessary as he penned his narrative. Either before he began writing or soon thereafter, he asked himself the question, "What is it that I want to say in these paragraphs?" For the introductory portion of the first lecture he answered his query by writing:

"1. That the usual explanations for southern defeat or failure are insufficient because they overlook the disintegration and collapse that took place behind the Confederate lines.

"2. That the war raised unexpected problems within the Confederacy which the southern people were unprepared to solve quickly enough, and that these problems involved the maintenance and organization of resources both for the armies and the people behind the lines.

"3. That the failure to find a solution for these difficulties so weakened and demoralized the civilian population that it was unable to give effective support to the armies; that the Confederacy had begun to crumble, or to break down *within,* long before the military situation appeared to be desperate.

"4. That these lectures will be concerned with the internal problems raised by the war and with the ineffectual though earnest efforts of the southern people to solve the problems.

"Then go on with the response to the call to arms to resist invasion, touch on light-heartedness as well as the sober-minded dread of war, and indicate, in passing, difficulties of procuring arms, munitions, etc., for new military organizations. But pass rapidly to first major problem—public finances of states and banking situation."

After writing an early draft of the last lecture, Ramsdell became his own critic and set down in longhand (a rare procedure, for he usually worked at his typewriter) a series of comments and questions.

"This third chapter needs a more detailed and documented description of the breakdown—from the fall of 1864 to the spring of 1865.

"A few descriptions of typical? local conditions.

"What about a brief reference to Gen. Bragg's inspection system set up early in 1864?

"Is it worthwhile to review the handling of each problem at the end of the chapter? Doubtful! Would not a description of conditions as indicated at top (above), be better?

"The whole chapter needs more effective, pertinent documentation."

The final draft of the lectures included a few citations, mainly to legislative acts and manuscript collections, but Ramsdell had every intention to support his statements by frequent footnotes. The abbreviation "Ref" appears scores of times in the margins, and occasionally the name of an author of a book or monograph stands as evidence that he would express his obligation to other scholars who wrote on the Confederacy. A willingness on the part of the present writer to attempt further documentation soon proved futile, and as other series of Fleming lectures have been published sans footnotes, citations were abandoned altogether. Certainly if anyone could write authoritatively on the Confederacy without resort to documentation Ramsdell could do so. Verification of sundry statements revealed a high degree of accuracy.

In the third lecture, Ramsdell used the personal pronoun "I" a few times. These he intended to delete from the published version, for among the marginalia he wrote, "Revise to eliminate 1st person." His wishes have not been followed in this premise, for it will always seem good to imagine that Ramsdell himself is still speaking. This intention to remove himself from the printed page is characteristic of the man. He was extremely modest and retiring. On a few occasions, he permitted the use of the personal pronoun in his published writings. Recall, however, a self-depreciating statement that embodied one such usage. In his presidential address before the Mississippi Valley Historical Association, he wrote: "It is time that such an examination should be made; and, since those more competent have not attempted it, I shall endeavor in this paper to direct attention to the question, even though I throw little new light upon it" (*Mississippi Valley Historical Review*, XVI [1929–1930], 152–53). Few have ever questioned the definitiveness with which Ramsdell handled the subject.

Many reasons have been assigned for the failure of the Confederacy to materialize in an independent republic. Some scholars have been content to list a number of them without emphasis; others have singled out the one reason for the Lost Cause, and in dogmatic fashion insisted that they had discovered the key to failure; still others have admitted a combination of

circumstances but have underscored a particular one.
Among the causes usually assigned are the northern
blockade, shortage of provisions, lack of mechanical
and military equipment, transportation difficulties,
disparity in manpower, faulty strategy, internal dis-
sension on the issue of state rights, monetary problems, inferior statesmen in important positions, a psy-
chological spirit of defeatism, and lack of popular
morale.

What was Ramsdell's conclusion after studying the
problem for thirty years? "If I were asked what was
the greatest single weakness of the Confederacy," he
wrote in his third lecture, "I should say, without much
hesitation, that it was in this matter of finances. The
resort to irredeemable paper money and to excessive
issues of such currency was fatal, for it weakened not
only the purchasing power of the government but also
destroyed economic security among the people. In
fact, there seems to be nothing vital that escaped its
baneful influence." Time and again Ramsdell recurred
to the financial question, either as a problem in itself
or as the key to others. Among the other reasons he
ranked transportation difficulty "next to finances in
its deleterious consequences," though he inserted a
cautious "perhaps" in his statement. He looked upon
"the industrial weakness of the South . . . [as] one
of the decisive factors in its defeat," gave much attention to illegal trade with the enemy, and introduced

various other elements that contributed to the Lost Cause.

It should be remembered, however, that Ramsdell emphasized internal problems—behind the lines. *"Could* . . . [southern people] have solved them if they had been able to anticipate them and if they had adopted other measures? That is a hard question," Ramsdell admitted, "but my present conviction is that only a series of miracles would have made it possible."

It may not be out of place in this prefatory note to set down a few of the highlights in the lecturer's career, awaiting, as Ramsdell would say, a better account by a "more competent" hand. Born at Salado, Texas, on April 4, 1877, he received his bachelor's and master's degrees at the University of Texas in 1903 and 1904. He was awarded the doctorate in 1910 by Columbia University, whither he was attracted for advanced graduate work by Dunning's enviable reputation as an impartial authority on the Reconstruction era. From 1906 until his death, Ramsdell taught history at the University of Texas and contributed prestige to its History Department by his sound scholarship. Summer session migrations to other schools supplemented his thirty-six years of service at the University of Texas: the University of Illinois, 1923 and 1926; the University of Colorado, 1924;

FOREWORD

Columbia University, 1927; the University of North Carolina, 1928; Western Reserve University, 1930; Northwestern University, 1932; the University of West Virginia, 1933; the University of Missouri, 1935; and Duke University, 1938.

While summer session appointments promoted research in various collections of historical materials, Ramsdell was instrumental in assembling at the University of Texas voluminous printed works and manuscripts in his special field. According to William C. Binkley, "he played a leading part in building up the Littlefield collection, which is now recognized as one of the outstanding collections in the nation for the study of southern history. A firm believer in the necessity of cooperation in making valuable source materials accessible to all workers, he took the lead in trying to plan for the interchange of the holdings of various depositories through the microfilm process" (*ibid.*, XXIX [1942–1943], 314–15).

Sundry historical associations honored Ramsdell with official positions. He served as president of the Southern Historical Association in 1936, as a member of its Executive Council, 1935–1939, and as a member of the Editorial Board of the *Journal of Southern History*, 1937–1940. The same services were performed for the Mississippi Valley Historical Association: as president, 1928–1929; as a member of the Executive Committee and its chairman for the six years following his presidency; and as a member of the

Board of Editors of the *Mississippi Valley Historical Review*, 1930–1933. From 1931 to 1934 Ramsdell
was a member of the American Historical Association's Executive Council. His interest in Texas history is indicated by twenty-eight years of service as
associate editor of the *Southwestern Historical Quarterly*, 1910–1938, and a longer period, 1907 until his
death, as secretary-treasurer of the Texas State Historical Association (see sketch by the writer in *Journal of Southern History*, VIII [1942], 445–47, from
which the last three paragraphs have been adapted
without the use of quotation marks).

Ramsdell's personal services to members of his profession were legion. Scholars everywhere turned to
him for aid in their research problems. Not the least
of his contributions was the generous amount of time
he gave to graduate students at the University of
Texas. For many years he taught courses in "The Old
South, 1783–1865" and "Civil War and Reconstruction."

Appended to the lectures here published is a bibliography of Ramsdell's writings. These include three
books (one of them in collaboration), two edited
works, twenty-two articles, six unpublished papers,
fifteen contributions to the *Dictionary of American
Biography* and two to the *Dictionary of American
History*, and some sixty book reviews. As a correspondent wrote to the writer recently, "I have never
known a man who knew so much and wrote so little."

A perusal of the bibliography, which seems to be reasonably complete, will probably reveal a larger heritage than many historians anticipated. Articles appeared every year or two, and book reviews averaged about two a year.

For a score of years, Ramsdell had been working on a history of the Confederacy. With the projecting of a ten-volume co-operative History of the South, of which he was serving as co-editor, his Confederacy study was designed as a volume in that series. Unfortunately, he had done little if any of the writing. The tragedy is that so much southern history accompanied him at his death on July 3, 1942. A member of the guild put it strikingly when he said: "Too much of caution, too much of honest care, too high a regard for perfection,—all these things held back his pen to the permanent impoverishment of American History." A penchant for thoroughness kept him ever at the task of searching for new materials. Ordinarily the impulse to put into print the results of his painstaking research was lacking. Yet he seldom declined an invitation to appear on the program of an association meeting, unless distance forbade attendance, for here was an assignment, an obligation.

While space does not permit an appraisal of Ramsdell's writings, attention may be called to his enthusiasm for the Southern Historical Association and the articles he published in its magazine. He saw in the founding of the Association an opportunity to

weld historians interested in the South into a conscious
unity and at the same time to stimulate greater pro-
ductivity. Ramsdell set a good example, not only by
accepting office in the organization, but also by ap-
pearing on its programs. Between May, 1936, and
August, 1937, he published three papers in the *Journal of Southern History.*

His analysis of "Some Problems Involved in Writing the History of the Confederacy" is an answer to
the question, why did Ramsdell not produce a magnum
opus years ago? At the same time it is prophetic of
the type of work Ramsdell would eventually have
written. As to scope and emphasis, he answered both
negatively and positively: "what we do *not* want is a
history that lays undue emphasis upon any particular
phase of the story, whether it be military operations,
or the political and administrative policies and difficulties of the Confederate government, or the socio-
economic conditions of the people. We want instead a
full, comprehensive, well-balanced and articulated account that will give due weight to all discoverable factors in the struggle of the Southern people for independence and their failure to achieve it. Without
sacrificing accuracy, it should have as much literary
charm as the writer is capable of imparting to it"
(*Journal of Southern History,* II [1936], 133–34).
He then proceeded to list, with proper integration,
illustrative contributions that scholars had made and
scores of gaps that remained to be filled before a his-

tory of the Confederacy could be written. In summarizing, Ramsdell observed that "anyone who, in the present state of our knowledge and available sources, attempts now to write a comprehensive history of the very complex life of the Confederacy must do a great deal of pioneer work for himself. We greatly need more good monographic studies based upon an exhaustive examination of sources. The very complexity of the field as a whole presents a difficult problem in the organization of the material. The evidence on many points is very scanty and in some cases is likely to remain so; in other instances, though fairly abundant, it is often technical or conflicting." Such problems, he admitted, were not peculiar to the epoch of the Confederacy; they "are always present to worry the historical investigator when he attempts to cover any large field of human endeavor" (*ibid.*, 147). With this evidence before us, added to Ramsdell's reluctance to write without outside stimulus, one can understand why he did not produce a history of the Confederacy.

Ramsdell's presidential address before the Southern Historical Association, "The Changing Interpretation of the Civil War," reveals the ripened scholarship of his mature years. It reviews the evolution from the apologias of contemporaries to the objective accounts of the twentieth century's critical school. It does more than assess the responsibility for the conflict and analyze the causes for the two great crises of 1860–1861, secession and civil war; it also weighs in the balance the results of the war, and finds them wanting. "Making all necessary allowances for our inability to weigh accurately the imponderables in the history of a great people," he wrote, "can we say with conviction that this war accomplished anything of lasting good that could not and would not have been won by the peaceful processes of social evolution? Is there not ground for the tragic conclusion that it accomplished little which was not otherwise attainable? Had the more than half a million lives and the ten billions of wasted property been saved, the wealth of the United States and the welfare of the people would not likely have been less than they are now. Perhaps some of the social and economic ills that have bedevilled us for the past fifty years would have been less troublesome" (*ibid.,* III [1937], 27).

"Lincoln and Fort Sumter" was read before a session of the Mississippi Valley Historical Association in December, 1935, and later at a dinner in Ramsdell's honor during the week that he inaugurated the Fleming Lectures at Louisiana State University. Greatly restricted in scope, nevertheless it should be ranked as one of his best studies. It shows that the author was a master in the art of marshaling evidence and of piecing together the fragmentary information from contemporaries into the plausible conclusion that Linoln, through ingenious strategy, "maneuvered the Confederates into firing the first shot in order that they, rather than he, should take the blame of beginning bloodshed" (*ibid.*, 285). When word came to Ramsdell that a member of the Association had said he could "shoot it full of holes," the Texan remarked with his usual chuckle, "That's just what the Confederates did to Fort Sumter. Perhaps my critic is a Rebel." He was not unaware of the fact that his critic was a Northerner.

It was a source of amusement as well as vexation to Ramsdell that southern historical scholarship was so belatedly recognized in the North, if not entirely ignored. As a mature scholar he was proud of the increasing volume of objectively written books and monographs emanating from the young historians of the South. Frequently, in the lobby sessions of association meetings, he voiced regret that their work was still largely unrecognized, and once, in a formal paper, he protested facetiously against the failure to accept valid new viewpoints in southern history: "It is a favorite dictum of many writers, more especially the Northern historians, that the emancipation of the African also set free the 'poor whites' of the South. Usually these writers seem to regard as 'poor whites' all who were not slaveowners. For something like a hundred years Southerners have been trying to make clear to Northerners the falsity of this definition and the difference between 'poor whites' and the great middle class of nonslaveholders. For some reason the misapprehension survives and it would be too weari-

[xx]

some to explain the distinction again" (*ibid.*, 23–24).
To those who did not know Ramsdell intimately, he appeared reserved and dignified. He possessed those qualities and more. The writer recalls his first glimpse of him at a meeting of the American Historical Association a dozen years ago. Ramsdell presided at one of the sessions, and the neophyte aspired to meet him after adjournment but was too scared to present himself. Not until after the establishment of the Southern Historical Association did he have opportunity to become acquainted with the Texas historian. He soon discovered that Ramsdell was a most kindly and genial gentleman, very approachable, and fully as interested in the novice as in the mature historian. He was an active participant in those story-telling hours of extracurricular sessions at association meetings, and his constructive contributions to them were surpassed only by the scholarly, cogent papers he read at the more formal sessions.

A word picture of the man comes from the pen of that skillful artist, Avery Craven. He said to the members of the Mississippi Valley Historical Association on April 23, 1943: "Genial and tolerant, interested and interesting, endowed with a keen sense of humor and a fine sense of honor, Professor Ramsdell had a talent for friendship possessed by few men. He could always take the time to visit, to tell a good story, or to give help to those who sought his counsel. He liked people. His chuckle was contagious; his reactions sincere and genuine. He inspired confidence and stirred affection. He was the kind of man whose passing leaves a permanently empty place" (Minutes of the Business Meeting, Cedar Rapids, Iowa, April 23, 1943).

It will always be pleasant for participants to recall that delightful April week in 1937 when Ramsdell inaugurated the Fleming Lectures. "Hokum College," an unofficial organization with activities off the campus, had planned a strenuous program, including trips to ante-bellum plantation homes in the Feliciana parishes, luncheons and dinners, midnight aftermaths, and a round of golf which the guest speaker won hands down. And then there was the inevitable initiation as a member of the faculty of the "College," with full authority to establish an Extension Center at Austin. Before his appointment to the "faculty" he was respected and honored; thereafter he was the lovable Ramsdell whom intimate friends cherished.

Various acknowledgments are gratefully recorded: to Mrs. Ramsdell for permission to publish the lectures; to Dr. Eugene C. Barker for providing a preliminary list of Ramsdell's writings and for helpful comment upon the Foreword; to Dr. Edwin A. Davis for useful suggestions relative to Ramsdell's career; to Dr. William C. Binkley for critical appraisal of the Foreword; to Dr. C. C. Crittenden for verifying quotations from materials in the North Carolina Historical Commission; to Dr. William D. McCain for verifying quotations from manuscripts in the Mississippi Department of Archives and History; and to Mrs. Kathryn Schuler for assistance in preparing the lectures for printing.

Baton Rouge, July 15, 1943   W. H. S.

CONTENTS

Behind the Lines in the Southern Confederacy

I
THE EMERGENCE OF WARTIME SOCIAL
AND ECONOMIC PROBLEMS

EVER since the collapse of the Southern Confederacy in the spring of 1865, historical writers and commentators have had much to say about the causes
of southern defeat. Southerners in particular have
stressed the greater strength of the North—its much
larger population and the heavier weight of its armies,
its more extensive industrial development and material
resources, its far greater financial strength, its possession of a navy with facilities for shipbuilding which
enabled it both to blockade the southern ports and to
keep northern waters open to the trade of the world
and to thousands of immigrant recruits for the Union
armies, and its ability through diplomatic pressure to
forestall foreign recognition of the Confederate government. And northern students of the subject have
generally agreed that these advantages were decisive.
Certainly, such a preponderance of resources would
seem to afford a sufficient explanation of the northern
victory.

[1]

And yet, if we look more closely into wartime conditions among the peoples of the two hostile sections, we find something more. For one thing, the North as a whole was exceedingly prosperous throughout the war, except for the first half of 1861; whereas the southern people, with a very few individual exceptions, sank rapidly into the direst poverty and suffered terrible privations. And this was true despite the fact that, during the ten years before the election of Abraham Lincoln to the presidency, they had been unusually prosperous. Nor was this suffering and poverty confined to the areas devastated by hostile Union armies; it was to be found in communities that never saw a Union soldier until after the surrender.

Another thing that becomes evident upon examination is that the North became, for that day, well organized for carrying on the war, while the South seemed unable to effect an efficient organization for dealing with the unforeseen exigencies of the struggle. To state it more precisely, the southern people—or, perhaps we should say their military and political leaders—were able to build an effective military machine, as far as fighting qualities were concerned, but they were only partly able to supply its needs in food and clothing and arms and transportation, and they failed completely to solve the problem of preserving the well-being and the morale of the civilian population behind the lines of the armies. Since it was upon these civilians that the strength of the armies in the last analysis depended, the failure to provide for them was fatal. But the problems of the civilian population were so extraordinarily difficult that it is not really surprising that they remained unsolved. And not only were they difficult; they were new to both the people and their leaders who were without either experience or organization for dealing with them. Lest you suspect that this is said in criticism of southern statesmanship, let me hasten to say that it would have required a miracle of statesmanship to solve these difficulties. And we cannot expect miracles. Some achievements on the battle front were very close to being miracles, but the difficulties which beset the people and the state and Confederate governments in the way of economic and financial and social problems, far beyond the sound of guns, were greater even than General Robert E. Lee faced across the wooded hills of Virginia. The northern people and their government also had their difficulties, and they, too, made mistakes; but the North was strong enough to recover from its errors and its society was better organized for dealing with the new problems which arose from the war. The South had not reached the same degree of economic, political, and social organization and was so much weaker that it could not afford to make mistakes.

We must remember that the South had always been primarily an agricultural region and its predominantly rural social organization retained many of the

[3]

characteristics of the early frontier. Its economic system was simple, based chiefly upon the growing of staple crops for export. Despite some evidences of wealth among planters and merchants, it was also largely a debtor section, or, at any rate, it had no great accumulations of cash or credit. Such manufacturing industries as it had established were still small and wholly incapable of supplying all the needs of the people. There were economic, geographic, climatic, and historical reasons for this condition, but we need not consider those reasons here. Its political organization was likewise simple, as befitted an agricultural society. Government was designed chiefly to maintain order among men and to protect the rights of property. Its proper functions, therefore, were limited to these things. Some states, it is true, had undertaken to aid such public improvements as canals or railroads or river levees. Some had encouraged or allowed banks to be established, while a few, such as Texas, had either forbidden them outright or had regarded them with suspicion. After a hard struggle most of them had begun to support public schools. But these people were strongly individualistic and believed that government should interfere as little as possible with private business beyond the collection of such taxes as were necessary to support a simple and economical government. The state governments had done but little in the way of the ameliorative social activities which have become so familiar in our day, for those

[4]

were held to be in the province of private philan-
thropy, not of government. The old political maxim,
"That government is best which governs least," re-
flected an attitude which, though by no means peculiar
to the South, was thoroughly characteristic of its people. The Federal government was held to be even more
limited in function than the state. It merely acted for
the Union of states in external relations and in such
internal matters as had been delegated to it by the
Constitution. While its economic and fiscal policies
could affect for better or worse the various groups of
citizens, as in the subjects of tariffs, public lands, taxes,
and appropriations, and while its authority rested
upon the individual within its own restricted sphere
of action, it was not to interfere with the social life or
the economic freedom of the individual. In those days
the citizen looked to his state, not to the Federal government, for the determination of his social, economic,
and political rights. This was not merely a matter of
law and custom; it was a system that fitted precisely
the relatively simple way of life in this agricultural
region, a political ideology which grew out of that
way of life.

The war was to change all this, for it was to raise
new and insistent problems too large and intricate to
be solved by private or local initiative. The imperious
necessity of solving them, if the people and their government were to be saved from invasion and conquest,
was to force the people and their responsible leaders

to discard their traditional ideas of laissez faire in private affairs and of the strictly limited functioning of government, and to turn to an increasingly centralized control over not merely military but likewise social and economic activities such as they had never anticipated and for which they had no precedent. What some of these problems were which arose behind the lines of the Confederate armies and what was done about them comprise the central theme of these lectures.

During the first weeks after the call to arms in the spring of 1861 little thought was given to future difficulties while gay young men were organizing themselves into companies under the proud and awe-inspiring names of "The King Cotton Guards," "The Spartan Band," "The Invincibles," "The Irrepressibles," "The Avengers," "The Raccoon Roughs," and the like. Though many tears were shed by mothers, wives, sisters, and sweethearts, they were as often tears of pride as of fear. After all, the war was to be short; with one glorious victory it would all be over, for, as soon as the "fanatical followers of Lincoln" should discover that the South was in earnest about its independence and was able to defend itself, they would desist. Besides, would not Great Britain and France intervene and break up Lincoln's blockade in order to procure the precious and indispensable cotton from the southern ports? The war might be over before there was a chance to have any fun with the

Yankees! In their enthusiasm for service more volunteers came forward than the combined efforts of the states and the Confederacy could arm and equip. Numbers of wealthy men furnished arms, equipment, and even horses to the poorer men in their commands; businessmen, lawyers, and farmers hurried into the army without taking time to make provision for carrying on their ordinary affairs; poor men left their families unprovided for under the promise and expectation that their dependents would be taken care of by well-to-do neighbors. Although they enlisted for twelve months, they expected to be home again before their term of service expired. It was with such eager and pathetic confidence that the southern people entered the dread portals of war!

But one threatening cloud already hung over the bright horizon, unnoticed except by the more thoughtful men. This was the problem of public finance, the most persistent difficulty that dogged the fortunes and hampered the efforts of the Confederate people during the long years of their desperate struggle. It had begun even before the Confederate government was formed. In November, 1860, the election of Lincoln and prospect of trouble caused bankers in both the North and the South to reduce their loans. Trade dropped off, business failures followed, especially in New York, and banks throughout the country began to suspend specie payments. That is, they refused to redeem their own outstanding bank notes in coin, but hoarded their gold to prevent a run on their gold reserves. In the southern states practically all the banks, except those of Louisiana and three in Alabama, quit paying out their specie. Their credit reduced and uneasy about the future, merchants canceled or cut down their orders for goods, and the trade of the southern ports fell to a very low point. In some states, as Alabama, Georgia, and Virginia, the governor or legislature authorized the suspension of specie payments by the banks in order to hold the gold for the use of the state government. While the secession movement was under way, all the southern state governments incurred heavy expenses in providing means of defense and they were obliged to continue these expenditures after the Confederate government was formed. Then, after the outbreak of hostilities, the Confederate officials depended upon the respective states to raise, arm, equip, and pay the volunteers until they could be mustered into the Confederate service. These emergency expenditures quickly drained away what small balances had been in the state treasuries and forced the states to borrow money. Naturally, the money market was in bad condition and state bonds, especially the bonds of seceded states, could not be sold in New York, even before the attack on Fort Sumter, except at a very heavy discount. The state authorities then turned to the local banks for money. Since all banks at that time depended upon state charters and state laws for existence—for there was no national banking system—they were more or less at the mercy of the state authorities. But if these banks were to take the state bonds and pay specie for them, they must be freed from their obligation to pay out that specie to the people who held their notes. Thus, the authorization given the banks to suspend specie payments to private holders of bank notes was generally a means of reserving that specie, usually gold, for the purchase of state bonds. Often the permission to suspend was conditioned upon the purchase of state bonds. Usually the bonds issued were apportioned among the banks in proportion to their capital. Of the specie received, the states paid out some for supplies bought outside the South. This gold went out, never to return. Some was paid to citizen contractors for supplies. Of this, some may have been redeposited in the banks, some went into the channels of trade, with a portion working its way out of the Confederacy. Some, perhaps, was hoarded. It is impossible to trace it. At any rate, in a short time the supply of specie was near exhaustion and, with more obligations piling up, legislatures were soon resorting to issues of state treasury notes based solely upon the credit of the states. These notes depreciated in value, of course. Although the Confederate government undertook to repay the states for their expenditures in raising troops and for the military supplies turned over to the Confederate War Department, since the Confederate treasury was itself without any appreciable amount of gold, these payments were made either in Confederate bonds or treasury notes which were not available until late in 1861.

Perhaps something should be said about the banks which did not suspend specie payments in the winter of 1860–1861. Governor Andrew B. Moore of Alabama, early in December, 1860, secretly asked the six banks of his state to suspend the payment of their gold in order that it might be reserved for the purchase of state bonds. Three suspended and three declined to do so, but all six bought the bonds, paying for them in coin. About the middle of September, 1861, the other three agreed to suspend specie payment in order further to assist the state treasury. The New Orleans banks did not suspend, partly because the state constitution forbade such action and the state banking laws of 1842 and 1855 imposed heavy penalties upon any bank which failed to redeem its notes in coin or which received and paid out other notes than its own, and partly because these banks had early taken the precaution to reduce their loans and note circulation and to build up their stock of gold. It has been estimated that there was about $25,000,-000, or a little more, of gold in all the southern banks on November 6, 1860. Of this amount the New Orleans banks alone held $10,000,000; by April 6, 1861, they held over $17,000,000 in gold. They were, thus, in a strong position; and they continued to pay out gold on demand until the middle of September, 1861, when their supply was reduced to a little more than $14,000,000. Christopher G. Memminger, the Confederate Secretary of the Treasury, noticed that Confederate treasury notes depreciated heavily in New Orleans because the banks could not, under Louisiana law, receive them or pay them out, and also because the notes of the New Orleans banks, being redeemable in gold, were generally preferred to the Confederate currency. He thereupon, September 11, 1861, appealed to the presidents of these banks to suspend the paying out of their specie and to receive government treasury notes, and urged the governor and other officials of the state to permit the suspension. This was agreed upon by the state officials and the banks. The banks with one exception suspended payments on September 16 and were relieved from the penalties of the law.

In August the Confederate Congress authorized the issue of $100,000,000 in Confederate treasury notes and the levy of a general war tax on property to provide for their redemption. The Confederacy set up no taxgathering machinery, and in expectation of hastening the collection, the states were permitted to assume the tax for their own citizens at a discount of 10 per cent if they paid it by April 1, 1862. With two exceptions, South Carolina and Texas, all the states took advantage of this provision, but to procure the money they either issued more of their own treasury notes or else required the banks to furnish the funds in exchange for other state bonds.

This dry recital of state financial expedients and bank policies has seemed necessary to explain two developments which were to have important consequences later: first, the rapid growth of state debts and the early exhaustion of state credit; second, the beginning, by the states themselves, before the Confederacy fell into the same policy, of a resort to heavy bond issues, the issue of irredeemable paper currency, and the dissipation of the small stock of gold in the banks. It was clearly a dangerous policy, as many Southerners well knew, and could be defended only as a necessary temporary expedient in the expectation of a short war. But, as the war dragged on and the Confederate treasury was driven by the scarcity of coin to the same paper money policy and began to issue huge amounts of unsalable bonds and irredeemable treasury notes, thoughtful men became alarmed. We shall see this depreciating currency aggravating every difficulty that beset both people and government.

Meanwhile, the course of business in general became erratic. The depression, which accompanied the futile discussions of compromise in the United States Congress and the secession movement in the Gulf states, caused southern merchants to cut down their orders for new goods. Whether there was much boycotting of northern-made articles is hard to say, though we know that there were threats of such reprisals. But when hostilities began, stocks of goods in many towns were already low. Then the blockade, while not yet very effective, discouraged importations. Business in the port towns fell off rapidly. On the other hand, there was a brisk demand for all sorts of army supplies—small arms, munitions, clothing, shoes, tents, blankets, cooking utensils, horses, wagons, leather goods, and foodstuffs. Agents and contractors for the army supply bureaus were busy; numbers of merchants whose ordinary business fell away became local quartermasters or purchasing agents for the army. Here and there men with an eye to profits in manufacturing articles needed for the army began to look about for capital with which to erect plants or enlarge existing establishments. The business of the railroads likewise suffered during the winter and many of them reduced their working force. Few were equipped for heavy business and, with the growth of government demands for transportation, they soon found themselves unable to handle the increased traffic. This was especially true of those which led toward the military frontiers in Virginia and Tennessee. In brief, while some lines of business were languishing, others were stimulated to great activity. Trade was suddenly shifted into new channels and the result was confusion.

The first concern of the people generally was the army of volunteers called out for their defense against invasion. The Confederate government, though aided by the states, strained its resources to arm and equip the soldiers; but the shortage of arms and other essential equipment seriously delayed the preparation

[13]

of a large proportion of the military units for active service in the field. The government at first did not even attempt to provide clothing for either men or officers. The privates and noncommissioned officers were required to provide their own clothing out of an allowance of "commutation money," about $25 per year, while the officers were expected to purchase their uniforms out of their salaries. All mounted men, except commissioned officers, were required to furnish their own horses for which they received an allowance of forty cents per day. These requirements threw the burdens back upon the soldier's family, except in rare cases where he was able to procure clothing in the vicinity of the camp.

The people at home were soon called upon for other assistance. The casualties at First Manassas in July and more particularly the epidemics of measles, typhoid fever, and other diseases which swept the camps of recruits emphasized the shortage of hospital facilities. Before the end of summer the army surgeons and medical purveyors were calling upon local authorities for help. Civilians formed hospital associations; and bands of devoted women, under the direction of physicians, began assembling or making medicines, bandages, sheets, and other hospital necessities and forwarding them to the army and base hospitals. In many cases these contributions were gifts; in others they were sold to the Medical Department or were made up from materials furnished by medical purveyors. There was much confusion, however, both in the preparation of these supplies, since it proved impossible to maintain standards of quality, and in the transmission of the articles to the hospital centers. In some cases the local organization wished its contributions to go to the soldiers from their own community or to those of their own state, even when paid for by the government—an arrangement which was difficult to carry out and which did not meet the approval of responsible government officials. In Georgia a Relief and Hospital Association which had been formed as a private corporation for the benefit of Georgia soldiers, sent agents to Virginia to erect a hospital and to see that contributions donated by the people of Georgia reached their own soldiers. In December, 1861, the legislature of Georgia appropriated $200,-000 for the aid and benefit of this organization. Several other legislatures also contributed funds for the support of similar hospital organizations. So scanty became the supplies of drugs and medicines, especially, that the Medical Department was forced throughout the war to rely largely upon the aid of these voluntary associations. The United States government placed all medicines and drugs, such as quinine, opium, and morphine, upon the contraband list so that both wounded Confederates and Union prisoners suffered untold agonies in the hospitals, while the Confederate surgeon and his staff tried to teach the people how to prepare medicines from the herbs of field and forest.

[15]

Before the end of the summer the Confederate quartermaster general began to look forward to procuring heavier clothing, blankets, shoes, and winter coats for the soldiers for the coming winter. Even this early the supply of these articles was short and the agents of the bureau were unable to find enough in the open market for the men already in the camps. Again the people at home were called upon to supply these needs from their scanty family resources. As the Quartermaster's Bureau began to work up in its own shops such materials as it had been able to procure, private donors were required to furnish their own materials. Complaints began to appear that wool and leather were unobtainable or that the market prices were beyond the reach of the poorer families or that the owners of wool or cotton yarn mills refused to sell except at exorbitant prices. Another difficulty frequently complained of was that consignments of clothing for individual soldiers or for particular companies in the army in Virginia never reached their destination. They were either held up somewhere along the railroads, were lost in transit, or were delivered to some other organization than the one for which they were intended.

The complaints against the railroads became vociferous and, apparently, for good reasons. The roads were, in fact, overcrowded with traffic and there was no proper supervision of shipments. It was charged that, since voluntary contributions to the needs of the soldiers were to be carried free, the road official deliberately shunted them aside in favor of traffic that paid. Speculators, it was alleged, could always get their goods shipped promptly. There were then no through lines from the Lower South to Richmond, but rather a series of short roads which made connection of a sort at various towns. Often the gauge of one road was different from that of the next so that cars could not be carried over to the next line. In such cases the goods had to be unloaded, carted across town, and reloaded on the cars of the second road. This made for delay and confusion. A newspaper correspondent in Richmond stated in October, 1861, that "several hundred carloads of voluntary contributions from different states for the army are at various stations *en route* to Richmond" awaiting the pleasure of the railway officials. Thus even before the war was well begun there were complaints about the scarcity of certain necessities, high prices, and difficulties of transportation.

It is easy to understand the scarcity of medicine or salt, for they had always been imported, but what of wool and leather which were produced in the country? The South was not a heavy wool-producing section. In 1860 it grew less than one sixth of the total crop in the United States, or a small fraction more than one pound per inhabitant in the Confederate States. Virginia, the largest southern producing state, alone contributed more than one fourth of the total, with Texas and Tennessee, next in order, together producing more than another fourth. But the chief wool-growing section of Virginia was soon in the hands of the Federals while the Texas wool was almost inaccessible, since there was no railroad from that state eastward and the route by sea was blocked. The cotton states, outside of Texas, produced very little, about three fourths of a pound per person. With the supply of raw wool so scanty and with only a few woolen yarn mills in the Confederacy, there is little wonder that warm woolen clothing for the soldiers shivering in the Virginia snows was hard to get. Families at home were cutting blankets out of carpets in that first winter of the war and the government was being urged to seize all the wool in order to get it out of the hands of speculators who had gone about the country buying up the small stocks available.

Leather was almost as scarce as wool, although there was a much larger potential supply, since cattle were far more plentiful than sheep. But tanners were not numerous, and butchers and commissary officers who slaughtered beeves for the army were careless about preserving the hides. The volunteers who wintered in Virginia were not too plentifully supplied with shoes and clothing, but their condition was luxurious compared with what it was to be in succeeding winters.

But our concern is chiefly with the civilian population. The war had hardly begun before they began to experience discomforts which passed quickly into actual privation. The blockade, though not as effective as it was to become later, greatly reduced all kinds of importations. While the neutrality of Kentucky during the first summer left a way open for goods to make their way south from the Ohio Valley, that resource was cut off by the early fall. Coffee was already so scarce by August, 1861, that substitutes, such as okra seeds and parched barley or corn, were being suggested in the newspapers for the "almost indispensable berry." By the end of October green coffee was quoted at fifty cents per pound in Savannah.

But the most spectacular rise was in the price of salt. This article, so common today that we take it as a matter of course, was essential then not only for the table and livestock but also for curing meats. There was no such thing during the days of the Confederacy as artificial refrigeration of meats; pork, especially, must be cured with salt. The southern states, like the western, had always imported their salt which came in cheap as ballast for ships. On May 2, 1861, a commission house in Savannah quoted imported salt at sixty-five cents per sack of 210 pounds. On October 30 a newspaper of the same town reported the price as running from $7 to $8 per sack. On November 18, the price having gone still higher and farmers and planters being unable to procure salt for use in curing their winter meat, Governor Joseph E. Brown of Georgia gave orders to the state commissary general in that city to seize a quantity of salt in the railway depot and pay the owners $5 per sack. About ten days earlier Governor Moore of Alabama, under authorization of the legislature, seized some 1,400 sacks in Montgomery for which he paid less than the market price. It was alleged in each case that the owners, referred to as "speculators," were about to send the salt out of the state. These remedies did not halt the upward tendency, if indeed they did not actually increase it, for within a month and a half the price went to $20 per sack. This salt scarcity existed all over the Confederacy and became one of the most troublesome problems of the people.

While the phenomenal rise in the price of salt was the most alarming, other commodities, too, were getting out of the reach of ordinary families. Wheat and flour, corn and corn meal, meats of all kinds, especially bacon, cloth of every kind, coarse or fine, all fabricated articles, iron, tin, copper, and the ordinary utensils of household or field or shop were rising steadily, if somewhat unevenly. Since this price rise was more rapid than the depreciation of the currency at this stage, it is fair to assume that the currency was not wholly responsible but that scarcity or fear of scarcity was an important factor.

There was grumbling at first, then irritation, and finally an outburst of rage. The belief was widespread that the high prices resulted from the activities of speculators and extortionists who cornered the market and held back their goods for exorbitant profits. It is very difficult to determine even approximately how much truth was in these charges. Evidently, if we can believe the statements of some responsible men, there was some truth in them. At any rate, the suffering populace demanded a remedy—either that the government seize the goods from the heartless speculators, as Governors Brown and Moore had done in the case of salt, or that the legislators impose heavy penalties upon the extortionists. Some of the legislatures responded. On November 11, 1861, Governor Moore approved a measure of the Alabama legislature entitled "An Act to Suppress Monopolies" which imposed a fine and imprisonment upon any person who should buy up livestock or any other commodity with the intent to create a scarcity in the market and obtain higher prices. Within a few weeks the legislatures of Florida, Mississippi, and Georgia passed similar acts. Several of these states also prohibited under heavy penalties any person from buying any commodity under the false representation that he was an agent or officer of the Confederate government or of a state— a shady practice which evidently was becoming common. That these laws were not enforced is clear enough from the continued rise and the even greater complaints of speculation and extortion as the war went on. In fact, Governor Brown admitted in November, 1862, that the law had been a dead letter in his state; that the unpatriotic and unchristian evils of extortion, engrossment, and speculation were still

[21]

rife; and that he had never heard of a conviction under the Georgia law.

Although all newspapers indulged in invectives
against the speculators and extortioners, many editors
and contributors now condemned the recent punitive
laws as futile and even tending to make prices still
higher. A citizen of Atlanta, for instance, writing
about April 1, 1862, pointed out that merchants were
compelled to pay high prices for their goods and could
not sell unless at some profit; they often incurred
heavy losses, such as that by Atlanta merchants between New Orleans and Atlanta of $100,000 worth
of goods, already paid for, which they did not expect
to recover. Nevertheless, we find Governor Francis
W. Pickens of South Carolina in the middle of April,
1862, proposing to the governors of North Carolina
and Georgia that the three states jointly fix maximum
prices upon "the necessaries of life." Governor John
Letcher of Virginia, also consulted, approved in principle but declined to act for want of authority. Governor Henry T. Clark of North Carolina laid the subject before the state convention, then in session, but
apparently without result. He did, however, by proclamation impose an embargo on foodstuffs, cotton,
and wool, except for articles purchased by the Confederacy or other state governments. This step, while
approved by many people of his own state, brought a
strong protest from Governor Letcher, whose people
were unable to get cotton they had bought in North

Carolina. Here, in fact, was a situation with which neither the people nor the public officials, who were painfully aware of its dangers, knew how to deal. The popular demand for the stabilization of prices was insistent, but could legislation accomplish it? Where was the line to be drawn between fair and unfair prices? Some articles were still fairly plentiful—why were they costing so much? Would it not be better to stimulate a greater production of the absolute necessities than to interfere with freedom of buying and selling? One factor in the situation we must not overlook: the Confederate currency had begun to decline steadily. By April, 1862, it had dropped to about sixty-five cents on the dollar, as measured by gold. But as prices of most necessities had run much higher than gold, it seems fair to assume that currency depreciation was not solely responsible for the rise in the cost of living.

Those who suffered most were the people of the towns and the poorer farmers, and of these the worst sufferers were the families of soldiers in the army. The falling off of trade in such cities as Charleston and New Orleans threw hundreds of men out of work and even those who had employment found that the cost of rents, clothing, fuel, and food was getting beyond their reach. In Richmond the influx of government officials, traders, and refugees from other sections of Virginia increased house rents enormously as well as the cost of provisions. John B. Jones, the Confederate

[23]

war clerk, whose famous *Diary* has long been a valuable source of information, stated as early as June 24, 1861, that the cost of board for himself and family was greater than his salary. By November he noted that the cost of dry goods, rents, and board had risen to more than double what they had been in the previous spring. Townspeople everywhere were dependent upon country produce for food, and the efforts of some of the authorities to regulate prices had the effect of causing farmers to keep back their bacon, corn, potatoes, butter, and other products. There was to be no relief for the poorer townspeople, except charity, while the war lasted.

The condition of the poorer families in the country, especially those whose men had gone to the army, was no better and in some cases must have been worse. It was hard for women and children to carry on the work of a farm with the heavy and clumsy tools which were in use in those days. Many of the poorer farmers used oxen for plowing and they were hard for women or boys to handle. Often, too, the oxen were impressed for beef by inconsiderate commissary officers. Consequently, on these farms scanty crops were planted and but little was raised. Even when the wife of a soldier was able to raise a little corn and forage, she had no money with which to buy clothing or shoes for herself and her small children, except what her husband was able to send her out of his pay of $11 a month. It had been expected, and in many cases promised, when these poor men volunteered for service, that their families would be looked after by their more fortunate neighbors; but this reliance upon private assistance had not worked well. While numbers of well-to-do families did not shirk the responsibility, others did. Not infrequently one planter who had remained at home, or his family if he also had gone to war, found it impossible to care for all the poorer families in the neighborhood. In many communities all were poor alike and there was no one to look to for help. As the first winter approached it became evident that some more equitable method of affording relief to the families in need must be devised and the legislatures which assembled in the fall and winter of 1861 were petitioned to provide the needed relief.

Between November, 1861, and March, 1862, the legislatures of Alabama, Arkansas, Florida, Mississippi, Tennessee, Georgia, and South Carolina passed acts for the relief of "indigent families of soldiers" in the service of the state or the Confederacy. These first measures usually provided for a state tax on property of all kinds, or else permitted each county court to levy a local tax, the proceeds of which were to be distributed among the needy families by the county authorities. The benefits were restricted to the families of volunteers in the Confederate or state service. The families of substitutes were excluded. All these measures left the assessment and collection of the special taxes and the administration and distribution of the funds to the county authorities. Each county, whether poor or wealthy, must provide all the relief for its own people. It was a county unit system. While a considerable amount of help was given under these acts during 1862, the results were spotted and irregular, for in those counties where crops had failed because of the drought that visited portions of the Gulf states that summer all alike were short of provisions. In some sections, too, poverty was so nearly universal that it was difficult to collect taxes of any kind. Even where the full amount was collected, there was not enough to provide for all who were in need.

If we may judge of conditions in some of these communities by the letters which flowed into the offices of governors, the plight of the poor was pitiful indeed by the latter half of 1862. The letters came from all classes, wealthy planters and poor farmers, some of whom were discharged soldiers, home for the first time in fifteen months. When a poor and all but illiterate farmer or wife of an absent soldier, not much accustomed to writing letters, sat down to write the governor of the state about the situation in the neighborhood, he had something to say or he would not have written at all. One interesting letter was from a well-known Mississippian, John F. H. Claiborne, former member of the United States Congress, author of *The Life and Correspondence of John A. Quitman* and later of *Mississippi as a Province, Territory and*

[26]

State. Claiborne wrote to Governor John J. Pettus
on August 4, 1862, from his home near the coast of
Hancock County, southern Mississippi. He stated that
because of the quality of the soil in that section not
more than one acre in a thousand was fit for cultivation. The people were poor and most of them depended upon the sale of wood, charcoal, and tar to
New Orleans in exchange for corn and other foodstuffs. After the fall of New Orleans that resource
had been cut off. Almost no corn would be raised, for
worms had ruined that planted on the alluvial lands
of the Pearl River and the drought had destroyed all
on the higher lands. He had expected a crop of 4,000
bushels on his own plantation, but would scarcely
make 1,500. After reserving enough to feed his Negro
hands, he was distributing what was left in small par-
cels of five bushels each to families in need. All would
soon be gone. In the previous year an epidemic of
charbon had carried off large numbers of horses, cattle, hogs, and sheep. He asked that permission be
granted to send wood and charcoal to the loyal people
of New Orleans in return for corn, meat, salt, shoes,
and clothing. Otherwise there was nothing for these
poor people to do but starve or go over to the enemy
in order to get food.

Here are some excerpts from a badly spelled letter,
innocent of punctuation, written on December 1,
1862, to Governor Pettus by M. M. Fortinberry, a
private soldier who returned on a furlough to his

home in Lawrence County on the Pearl River in south central Mississippi:

first we have failed to make a crop   poor men have been compelled to leave the army to come home to provide for their families . . . we are compelled to ask you for protection untill we can provide for our families   to stay in the army at eleven dollars per month and if we live to get home pay sixty dollars for a sack of salt if we can get it at that and corn at two Dollars per bushel . . . we are poor men and are willing to defend our country but our families first and then our count[r]y . . . their is no use to depend on the charity of our neighbours for they are all in our condition. . . . This is the general feeling of the community in which I live determined to make a crop if we can   now we ask you to protect us while we work our farms   your immediate attention is invited to this note and an answer returned as we are forced to this or starve . . .

The request for protection suggests that this soldier and some of his neighbors had not returned to the army at the expiration of their furloughs and that others were deserters.

Another letter from W. H. Hardy in a neighboring county, dated December 2, 1862, informed Pettus:

There is now in the county much suffering amongst the poorer classes of Volunteers families—much suffering for want of *corn and salt*. Owing to the drought

last summer the corn crop was a failure in this section
of the State except on the rich Bottom Lands owned
principally by the wealthier planters. . . . These
have made a superabundance of corn, and if it could
be properly distributed through the Co. there would
be enough to prevent suffering. But the *Demon spirit*
of speculation which is doing our Government and
our people more injury than the Yankees, has taken
hold of them, and they are consequently holding their
corn at $2.50 per Bu.—many holding back, saying
they will get $3.00—thus placing the corn out of the
reach of the poor women who are dependent on their
Husband's $11 pr month, earned in the army, for
means to purchase with. Then to deal with facts. The
sufferers are here. The families of 600 volunteers are
here a large majority of whom are very poor people.
They are suffering for Bread. *The Bread is also here,*
but owing to the High price is beyond the reach of
these poor people. Now the question is—Can the
Legislature place it within their reach?

Again—the Confederate Government has exempted all Tanners and Shoemakers from military
service. There are in this County three Tan Yards at
each of which Leather and Shoes are manufactured,
—Yet not a pair can be bought by a citizen in the
county—and daily the wife or child of some Soldier
is turned off barefooted with the plea that "We work
for Government." Has the Government a right to
monopolize this department of trade to the utter ex-
clusion of all who are not in the service of the Gov-

[29]

ernment, even the wives and children of Volunteers[?] . . .

Again, the entire monopoly exercised by the government over our Rail Roads is working a very great Hards[h]ip upon the country. To illustrate—upon my return from the army in Va. I visited the families of the Volunteers of my Company and found them in many instances suffering for the want of salt etc. I made a hasty trip to Vicksburge where I was fortunate enough to procure Salt and Sugar &c for them. This purchase was made about a month ago, yet that Salt after paying 36 cts a lb for it out of money earned by soldiering at $11 per month is still *lying at Vicksburge* for want of transportation—and these poor women and children are stil without meat. The agent at Vicksburge told me the Road was under control of the Government and hence could only transport such articles as the Government agts directed.

In the name of God, I ask is this to be tolerated? Is this war to be carried on and the Government upheld at the expense of the Starvation of the Women and children . . . ? I hope not . . . Another army besides that in the field must be supported—*the army at home* . . . Their preservation and their comfort are as essential to our success as that of our Soldiers in the field . . .

These letters are from southern Mississippi, but similar portrayals of the privations and suffering of the families of the poor can be cited for other states, particularly northern Alabama and Georgia and western North Carolina. And there was an ominous note in many of them: men in the army, learning of the plight of their families, were coming home, with or without leave, to look after them and then, seeing how desperate the condition was, were not inclined to return to their commands. Desertion was beginning. Poor men still in the army were threatening to come home if something were not done to give more relief to their dependents.

Along the Mississippi River another dangerous situation had developed. The Federals took New Orleans in the late spring and pushed up to Baton Rouge and beyond and out into the rich planting country west of the river. Grant's army fought its way down through western Tennessee into northern Mississippi, threatened the rich plantation lands of the Yazoo Delta, and occupied eastern Arkansas. Livestock, cotton, and provisions were seized, houses plundered, and Negro slaves enticed away. The slaves in adjoining counties were becoming restless and unmanageable by the white women and children who remained on those plantations from which the men had gone to the Confederate armies. In April, 1862, the Confederate Congress enacted its first conscription law, taking into military service all able-bodied men between the ages of eighteen and thirty-five. Early in the summer the governor of Mississippi, under a recent act of the legislature, ordered a draft of the militia for service with the Confederate army. This would take away what able-bodied men were left. Fear seized upon the women left on the lonely plantations. Petitions poured in upon Governor Pettus begging him to exempt from military service at least one able-bodied man on each plantation, lest the Negroes get out of hand. A woman, signing herself merely "A Planter's Wife," wrote from Warren County, May 1, 1862, beseeching him to follow the good example of Governor Thomas O. Moore of Louisiana in leaving at least one man on each plantation. Many plantations, with large numbers of slaves, were without a white male old enough to shoulder a gun, and many were without meat. The Negroes could be controlled only so long as they had plenty of food. When this was gone "do you suppose they will hesitate to do that which the poor in many cities are on the eve of doing to secure the staff of life? Do you think that *then* woman's hand can keep them in check?" Besides, the country would have to depend upon the plantations for all the meat, grain, and forage for both the army and the people. An old man, Benjamin W. Bedford, wrote from Panola County on May 3, 1862, that unless overseers could be retained on the plantations in that section there would be no corn raised on the rich bottom lands. He himself would make 10,000 bushels and would have 250 hogs to slaughter if his overseer could remain. If every man were taken away the result would be disastrous, for it was to this fertile section of the state that the people and army must look for food.

Another, C. L. Buck of Issaquena County, in the lower Yazoo Delta, wrote a month later that along Deer Creek there was a continuous string of plantations the length of the county with not enough white men left to perform patrol duty. To take away more of the men would be to invite insubordination among the slaves and hazard the lives of every family there. If enough men could be left to keep the Negroes at work, enough corn could be grown to feed an army; but unless the slaves were kept under control no crops would be raised and starvation would result. Some of the Negroes had already run away to the Yankees.

There were scores of such letters, some of them written by frightened women growing more and more uneasy as the Federal armies approached or threatened. Similar appeals must have gone to members of the Confederate Congress, not only from this area but also from other planting sections in like danger, as on the coasts of Georgia and the Carolinas. In the light of this situation it is not so hard to understand why the Confederate Congress, when it came to extend the exemption provisions of the Conscription Act in October, 1862, should exempt one man, where there was no other man not liable to military service, for each twenty Negroes on a plantation. The real purpose of this act, so widely condemned, was not only to give protection to women and children but also to see that grain crops were planted and harvested by the slaves for the benefit of both the army and the

[33]

people generally. But this law, which was repealed in February, 1864, caused more discontent among the poor, who felt that it was a discrimination in favor of the well-to-do planter, than any other action of the government.

The necessity for growing a sufficient food supply had been called to the attention of the people in the winter of 1861–1862. The cotton crop of 1861 had been a large one, and as very little of it could be marketed, it was still on hand when planting time arrived in the spring of 1862. A movement then began, supported by all the newspapers and by the cotton planters themselves, to reduce radically the planting of cotton for 1862 and to increase the planting of corn, wheat, and other food crops. It was argued that another cotton crop would merely increase the supply on hand without adding to the total value, since the price would fall without a market; it could not be eaten; and its accumulation at exposed points would tempt the enemy to make raids. If, on the other hand, the South raised plenty of food for the army and the people at home, the blockade would do little harm. Food would win the war! During the winter mass meetings of farmers and planters passed resolutions promising to cut their cotton acreage to one half or one third of the customary amount and to plant more grain, potatoes, peas, beans, sorghum, and other food and forage crops. That most planters faithfully carried out the program is evidenced by many local reports and the fact that the cotton crop of 1862 was estimated at around one third of that of the previous year. But, while some planted no cotton at all, or only enough for seed, others refused to reduce their crop. And the grain crop was not as large as expected, partly because of the drought and partly because so many of the workers of the small farms were absent in the army. The wheat crop in northern Georgia and Alabama and eastern Tennessee was about one third of what had been expected.

Meanwhile, the price of cotton on the world market began to soar. Blockade-runners worked out a technique for slipping through the Union vessels off the harbors of such ports as Wilmington, Charleston, and Mobile; exporting corporations were chartered by South Carolina and other states; an overland trade developed between the interior cotton section of Texas and the Mexican border; and an illicit trade began across the military lines between cotton growers and northern buyers. These facts seem to have decided some planters to increase their cotton acreage for 1863. Moreover, the legislatures of certain states, like Mississippi, Alabama, and South Carolina, authorized the formation of cotton loan banks or associations in order to permit planters in need of funds to borrow money on their cotton, and perhaps this action caused planters to think of increasing their cotton production. But whatever the reason there was evidence that the voluntary method of reducing the cotton crop in favor of grains was about to break down. In consequence, a movement began to pass legislation limiting cotton production in favor of grain. It seems to have been supported not only by patriotic planters but also by the poorer people whose only hope of avoiding a food shortage and extravagant prices was in a greater production of grains. The legislature of Arkansas, a state that was peculiarly exposed to invasion, led the way in March, 1862, by prohibiting under heavy penalties of fine and imprisonment the planting of more than two acres of cotton to a field hand. In December, 1862, the legislature of Alabama imposed a tax of ten cents per pound upon all cotton grown on any farm or plantation in excess of 2,500 pounds of seed cotton per hand; while the Georgia legislature prohibited the planting of more than three acres of cotton per hand, and requested Governor Brown to ask the governors of other states to induce their legislatures to take similar action in behalf of the common cause. In February, 1863, the South Carolina legislature limited the planting of cotton in that state and in March the Virginia assembly strictly limited the planting of tobacco.

But the reduction of cotton acreage was not the only measure adopted to increase the supply of food. Another was the movement to stop the distillation of grain and other products into intoxicating liquors. Despite the efforts of the evangelical churches, Southerners had consumed a very considerable quantity of

[36]

liquors before the war, each section after its habit—
wines along the coast, fiery corn whisky in the interior,
mellow bourbons in Kentucky and other portions of
the Upper South. But most of these liquors, except
those of Kentucky, had been imported—the wines
from Europe, the corn whisky from the Northwest—
and they had been very cheap. The blockade cut off
the supply from outside and prices rose rapidly. These
high prices induced numbers of small distilleries to
be set up for the relief of the thirsty at large profits.
By the fall of 1861 it was noticed in some communities where there was a shortage of grain that the dis-
tillers were using large quantities of corn and endan-
gering the supply of bread. Complaints began to
appear in the newspapers and in the mail of governors
and other public officials urging that the legislatures,
or the governors if legislatures were not in session,
put a stop to this use of grain. But the hospitals made
use of alcohol both as a stimulant in certain types of
cases and as a solvent in the preparation of various
medicines. Care should be taken, therefore, not to interfere with the needs of the government or the medical profession. Apparently the first positive action
was taken by the governor and council of South Carolina when, on February 20, 1862, they adopted resolutions prohibiting, under penalty of a fine up to $10,-
000 and imprisonment up to one year, the distillation
of spirits from corn, rye, wheat, barley, or other grain,
but provided that a distiller might be licensed under

[37]

heavy bond to distill a fixed amount of spirits to be sold only to the Confederate government or to the state. Virginia followed with a similar act on March 12 and Arkansas with another on March 19. The state convention of North Carolina also passed an ordinance prohibiting distillation in that state. The governor of Georgia had ordered all stills closed except those given special permission by him to make alcohol or whisky for army hospitals and medical purposes. In November and December, 1862, the legislatures of Georgia, Alabama, and North Carolina passed prohibitory laws, saving only the needs of the Confederate government or the state authorities and then by permission of the governor. It is interesting to note that the North Carolina act included among the articles whose distillation was prohibited not only the several grains but also peas, peanuts, oats, Chinese sugar cane and its seed, syrup, molasses, rice, dried fruits, and potatoes, which may indicate that the North Carolinians had either greater native resourcefulness or wider experience in concocting their drinks. Despite the heavy penalties imposed, these laws were but partially, and unequally, enforced. That story will come later. But the passage of these prohibitory laws is an interesting illustration of another complete reversal of traditional or accustomed policy in view of public necessity under stress of the struggle for existence. It should be borne in mind that, although there had been much complaint of drunkenness both in the

[38]

army and among civilians, and doubtless the desire to lessen this evil was a factor in bringing about their passage, the laws were aimed primarily at the protection of the food supply.

While the state governments were endeavoring to frame legislation to deal with the new economic problems created by the war, the Confederate government refrained from legislation of this character. According to the southern political philosophy, its powers were limited by the Constitution, whereas the several states, though not the legislatures, were sovereign. But the Confederate Congress had, under its constitutional authority to wage war and to regulate commerce, enacted certain laws which did affect the customary liberties of the individual citizen. The most important were the conscription acts of April 16 and September 27, 1862, making all able-bodied white men between the ages of eighteen and thirty-five under the first law, and up to forty-five under the second, liable to military service. These acts were modified by the exemption provisions of April 21 and October 11, 1862, by relieving from military service those whose civil occupations were held to be of special value to society. The sale of cotton to the enemy was provided against by an act of May 21, 1861, which prohibited the exportation of cotton except through the Confederate ports or through Mexico and was made more explicit by another of April 19, 1862. Twice in 1862 Congress authorized the President to suspend the privilege of the writ of habeas corpus, once in February and again in October, but in each case for a short period. This legislation, while it all affected the customary liberties of the people, was not of the same character as that of the states and shows that up to this point the general government had not attempted to deal directly with the domestic problems of the people behind the lines. That was left to the states.

If we look back at what had been done during less than two years of war, we find that the southern people had already abandoned their habitual laissez-faire concepts of the functions of government. They had required their state authorities to attempt to check the dangerous increase in the cost of living. Although there was common-law precedent for the measures taken and although they were unsuccessful, they mark a decided break with earlier practice in the South. The relief laws for the benefit of indigent families of soldiers resulted, doubtless, from considerations of policy as well as humanity, for the responsible leaders well understood that otherwise the men of these families could not be kept in the ranks of the army; but the acts themselves were on a scale never before attempted in this country. More striking, in some ways, were the restrictions placed upon the customary rights of farmers and planters to plant what they pleased. The prohibition laws, another radical departure from custom, although intended primarily to conserve foods, seem to have had as a secondary purpose elimination of intoxicating liquors. And the state governments were beginning other unprecedented activities which have not yet been mentioned: they were taking up the manufacture or purchase of certain absolute necessities for the use of their people. This was to lead them into fields hitherto reserved to private business. Of course it was imperious necessity that brought them to it, but the mere fact that they did these things and were supported by their people in doing them shows that long-cherished traditions and laws and political principles are likely to be set aside when the general public interest seems to demand a change.

In the next chapter we shall watch the strengthening of this type of control by the states and to some extent by the Confederate government as conditions grew more desperate during the weary days of 1863 and 1864.

II

EXPERIMENTS IN POLITICAL CONTROL

WHEN the fateful year of 1863 arrived, the condition of the mass of the people behind the military lines was far worse than it had been a year earlier. The value of both Confederate and state currency was declining rapidly, for already the paper dollar of the Confederate treasury was down to thirty cents. In some quarters it was worth less and even state currency and the notes of the suspended banks were preferred. Gold and silver coin had virtually disappeared. As the purchasing power of the currency fell off, prices had risen. But commodity prices were not measured wholly by the decline of the currency, and the rise was very irregular. Articles which must be imported, such as coffee, tea, medicines, fine shoes, and the better grades of cloth were at from ten to twenty times their prewar prices. Salt, which was still being brought in on blockade-runners and was also being produced in Virginia, Alabama, and along the seashore, varied in price from $8 and $10 to $50 per sack of 200 pounds, and sometimes retailed at fifty cents a pound. The lower prices were those at which salt from state works was sold by state agents to the people; but since the states were unable to provide enough to meet the demand the private dealers were able to get the higher prices. One article that became an absolute necessity for the mass of the country people was cotton or woolen yarn. Cloth of all kinds was very scarce, for the small cotton and woolen mills were wholly unable to supply the demand. Some of these mills spun yarns but did no weaving, and had always sold their yarn to the cloth mills. With cloth so scarce and expensive, thousands of families turned to the primitive hand loom and the making of homespun. But when they tried to buy yarn from the little yarn mills or the merchants, they found prices beyond their reach, from $8 to $10 per bunch. They could not spin their own cotton yarn because the raw cotton must first be carded and they had no cards. Shoes were selling at from $10 to $25 per pair, according to the quality and locality, and poor families were going without them, even in the winter.

But it was the inflated prices of foodstuffs that caused the greatest privation and indignation. The wheat crop of 1862 was disappointing even in Virginia which had long been a large producer of this grain. The Confederate Commissary General, Colonel Lucius B. Northrop, estimated early in November, 1862, that the Virginia wheat crop was less than a third of the normal amount. Most of that of middle Tennessee was lost to the enemy, while the crop in

Georgia, Alabama, and other states of the Lower South was either badly damaged by rust or ruined by drought. Prices soared. But the southern people were not obliged to eat flour bread; many of them had been accustomed to corn bread and they could turn to that exclusively if need be. The price of this great southern food staple, however, had also gone to unheard-of heights, especially in cities like Richmond where all prices were high, and in the more remote sections of the country where crops had been short and where the poorer people were the least able to buy it. The prices of corn and corn meal varied so much, from $3 to $10 per bushel for corn and somewhat higher for meal, that the differences can be accounted for only by the difficulty of transporting it from those regions where it was plentiful to those where it was scarce.

As far as food was concerned, the planters of the interior who had good soil and slave labor to care for the crops, and who were safe from the enemy, had suffered little. But even the well-to-do planters were having difficulty in procuring clothing and in replacing worn-out household or farming utensils. The poor everywhere were having a hard time and faced starvation almost daily, whether they lived in towns, subsisting on wages or salaries, or whether they lived on the little farms back in the hill country. And yet there seems to have been enough food to supply all the people if it could have been properly distributed. Indignant men and women were calling attention to this fact and were asking grimly what the authorities proposed to do about it.

It was inevitable that discontent should be felt and voiced by those who suffered undue privations, especially when they saw their children go without shoes, warm clothing, meat, and sometimes without bread. From every section of every state letters were pouring in to the governors calling attention to the exorbitant cost of the simplest articles of food and pointing out the perilous situation of those families which were dependent upon a soldier's pay or upon the small wages which women and children could earn near home. Not infrequently a letter contained an ominous warning that men would not stay in the army while their families suffered. Relief measures enacted by various legislatures in the previous winter and even in the fall of 1862 fell short of their objectives, partly because taxes for relief purposes were not fully collected, and partly because of the lowered purchasing power of the currency. A new factor in the situation was President Lincoln's Emancipation Proclamation. It had the effect of making the war, which, on the southern side, began as an effort to save the people from invasion, now appear more as one to save the property of the slaveowner.

Here are portions of two letters to Governor Zebulon B. Vance of North Carolina written early in

1863, both of which refer to the consequences of the poorer people's inability to buy food. The first came from R. D. Hart, an old man living at Oxford, Granville County, in the northern part of the state. It runs:

There is a degree of Penury & Want in this county, & others no doubt that is truly distressing & under existing circumstances I do contend that our Governor & Legislature should interfere. I am ready to concede that it is a matter of great dellicacy for *you* or our Legislature to sett a price on the property of Individuals, but not half so much so as to drag the Persons of our Citizens from their peaceful homes and price their labor at Eleven Dollars *pr* month, while their families are suffering the extremes of Privation and Want. I shudder now & then when I look forward to the probable consequences. There is no doubt an ample sufficiency of Corn in this county for its consumption; but holders can't be moved to sell for less than the most exhorbitant prices & many women & children are entirely without. Now just let this news reach our Soldiers in the Army whose families are thus oppressed, & I should not be surprised to hear any day that many of them had laid by their arms and marched off home. Surely no one could blame them. A price should be established for every article of food & those having to spare should be compelled to sell at such rates . . . [as] our Legislature might deem reasonable. No man can give a sufficient reason why corn should be or sell for more than six Dollars any where within this state. . . .

The second letter, written in an angry mood and badly misspelled, is from Bladen County, on the Cape Fear River in the southern part of North Carolina:

. . . the time has come that we the comon people has to hav bread or blood & we are bound boath men & women to hav it or die in the attempt   Some of us has bin travling for the last month with the money in our pockets to buy corn & tryd men that had plenty & has bin unable to buy a bushel holding on for a better price   We are willing to gave . . . two Dollars a bushel but no more for the idea is that the Slave oner has the plantations & the hands to rais the brad stufs & the comon people is drove of[f] in the war to fight for the big mans negro & he at home making nearly all the corn that is made & then because he has the play in his own fingers he puts the price on his corn so as to take all the soldiers wages for a fiew bushels   . . . it is not our desiar to organize & commence operations for if the precedent is laid it will be unanimous but if ther is not steps taken soon nessesity will drive us into measures that may proove awful   we dont ask meet on fair terms for we can live on bread   perhaps it would be better for you to esue your proclamation that no man should sell in the state at more than $2 pr bushel   you no best & if you cant remedy Extosan [extortion] on the staff of life we will & we as your subjects will make Examples of all who Refuse to open there barn Doors & [will] appoint other men over there farms who perhaps will hav better harts   we no that this is un-

[47]

lawful at a commontime but we are shut up   we cant trade with no body only Just those in the confedersy & they can perish[—]all those that has not [—] & it seems that all harts is turnd to gizards. . . .

Despite its crudities this anonymous letter expressed very clearly and pointedly what must have been passing through the minds of thousands of angry men.

The clamor over the high prices, the frightful cost of living, rose higher and extended from one end of the Confederacy to the other. Newspapers joined in the universal execration of the extortioner and speculator and turned as savagely as the poorer men upon the planter who held his corn or bacon for the top price. But the newspaper owner himself raised the subscription price of his paper and of the scanty advertisements which it carried. He could not do otherwise and continue to publish, for he paid more now for paper, printer's ink, and the wages of his employees. There was nothing that did not rise in price, except the wages of private soldiers and of contract laborers. A group of women in Salisbury, North Carolina, some of whom were working at pitifully small wages in the government clothing shops, were unable to procure food for themselves and their children at prices they could pay. In March they invaded a number of stores, offered the merchants "government prices" for flour, bacon, salt, and molasses, and when they were refused took the articles, apparently with the approval and backing of a number of townsmen.

One of them, Mary C. Moore, in a letter to Governor Vance explaining the affair, said:

We are all Soldiers Wives or Mothers. . . . how far will eleven dollars go in a family now when meat is from 75 to $1 00 pr pound, flour $50 pr bll, wood from 4 to 5$ pr load, meal b[ran] 4 an[d] 5 dollars pr bushel, eggs 50 to 60 cts pr dz . . . Molasses $7 00 pr gal? . . . We are willing and do work early and late to keep off starvation which is now staring us in the face. But the Government only allows us 50 cents a pr for lined pants and 75 cents for coats and there are few of us who can make over a dollar a day and we have upon an average from three to five helpless children to support. . . . Now Sir how we ask you in the name of God are we to live?

On the morning of April 2 occurred the famous bread riot in Richmond, the Confederacy's capital, when a mob of more than a thousand women and a few men gathered in Capitol Square and marched down Cary and Main streets, entered a number of stores, and took provisions and clothing. Only after speeches by Governor Letcher, several Congressmen, and finally President Davis, urging them to disperse, did they finally go away. The Richmond newspapers kept silent about the affair until northern papers got the news and made much of it; then they belittled it as the work of vagabonds and criminals. But it is evident that most of the crowd were not of that class. A little later in the same month small risings of a similar character took place in Augusta, Milledgeville, and Columbus, Georgia, but were soon dispersed.

But the "speculators" and "monopolists" were not the only persons whose antisocial practices aroused vituperation. Army purchasing officers began early in the war, under authority from the War Department, to impress needed supplies when the owners refused to sell at the rates offered, and the practice became common as prices rose and the funds in the hands of these officers became insufficient to cover the open market costs of the articles they were expected to procure for the army. In fact, the quartermasters and commissaries were nearly as indignant at the rise of prices as were the people, and frequently expressed the belief that the greed of speculators, merchants, manufacturers, and planters was responsible for the depreciation of the currency. Many of them fell into the habit of taking what they wanted and paying much less than the prevailing price; and farmers who had themselves berated the merchant who charged an outrageous price for salt or a pair of shoes, choked with wrath when an impressing officer refused to pay them what they asked for bacon, corn, or horses. Another practice of some impressing officers was to sweep the country of supplies near a railroad and leave more remote sections, whence transportation was difficult, untouched. In areas near the armies, as in Mississippi or on the main lines which supplied large forces, the higher military officials often either impressed all the services of the roads or made contracts which effectually monopolized them for military purposes with the result that private parties could not get shipments. This was especially hard upon those communities which in times of scarcity could not obtain shipments of corn, salt, or other articles for the relief of their people. Only the rich speculator, it was believed, was able, through bribery of the railroad officials, to get his goods through. The truth of the matter was that the railroads, which were never built for such traffic as was imposed upon them and which were seldom able to repair broken engines or cars without much delay, were wholly unable to handle all the goods which were brought to them. In consequence, their warehouses and those of the government were generally filled with bulky goods, such as corn and forage, which sometimes remained unmoved until it was ruined. This, too, enraged needy people who saw the waste and could not understand it.

Desertion from the army had already become a serious problem. The dangers, hardships, and often the dull monotony of life in the camps had much to do with the decision of men who had fought well to leave the service. But the evidence shows that thousands of them had become resentful at the unrelieved privations of their families at home. This was especially true of men from the poorer sections of the back country, and it seems significant that the largest percentage of desertion was among the troops from those

[51]

regions. Especially did they resent the terms of the Exemption Act of October 11, 1862, which seemed to small farmers to cover everybody except themselves, but more particularly they took exception to those clauses which exempted the owners of large numbers of livestock and one man for every twenty slaves. It must be admitted that much of the grumbling over these exemptions came of mere prejudice and inability or unwillingness to understand that certain civilian services must be carried on for the sake of both the army and the people, and that Congress had endeavored to work out a selective service plan which would strengthen the military defenses and develop the resources of the country for carrying on the war. But the poorer men felt that they were being discriminated against and the old prejudices toward the wealthier classes flamed out in the well-known phrase which summed up their point of view so aptly: "It's a rich man's war and a poor man's fight." Was a cleavage on class lines about to be added to the other troubles of the hard-pressed young Confederacy?

Not all deserters had deliberately run away from their commands. Some had gone home on furlough and for various reasons decided not to go back. Some were paroled prisoners of war who, when finally exchanged, decided they had had enough of fighting. But whatever the reason, deserters could not safely stay at home where the conscript enrolling officers or other officials could find them. Consequently they spent much of their time hiding out in the woods, slipping back home at night for food; or else they banded together in remote places for resistance to the squads of Confederate soldiers or state militia sent after them. Of course, under such conditions they could not cultivate crops, so little food was raised in those communities where they congregated. Pitched battles, on a small scale to be sure, had begun to occur in the mountain regions during this winter of 1862–1863, and these conflicts were all that was needed to make the deserters outlaws. They joined forces with Unionists from eastern Tennessee and southeastern Kentucky, became openly hostile to the Confederacy, plundered and sometimes murdered the loyal citizens, and defied the authorities. Every governor sought loyally to stop desertion and to aid in the arrest of the "skulkers," either through the use of the state militia directly or, as in North Carolina, where Vance permitted Confederate officers to use the militia as a posse after the chief justice of that state had declared the governor had no authority to arrest deserters from the Confederate army. Although the governors were able to catch some of these men, they were never able to break up the combinations which had gathered in the mountains.

The state militia, however, was not always useful nor even completely loyal. Made up in part of men and boys, over and under the conscript ages, it contained also numbers of others within the military ages who

[53]

had enrolled themselves in state service in the hope of escaping the more rigorous discipline and dangers of the Confederate armies. Volunteer companies of "home guards" had been organized ostensibly to render local patrol service, often with the understanding that they were not to be taken out of their own county. But if we may believe what some of their own officers said of them, the militia was often a poor lot as far as any effective service to the cause was concerned. In March, 1863, Governor Letcher informed the Virginia general assembly that five sixths of the "state Line" had deserted, taking their arms and munitions away with them because they were about to be transferred to the Confederate service. A few days later the legislature, by joint resolution, abolished the organization. In Mississippi before the end of 1862 the militia was reported as discontented, half-mutinous, and depleted by desertion. Because of the threat of Federal attacks from the north and against Vicksburg, Governor Pettus ordered a militia draft which was more stringent than Confederate conscription. Even owners of twenty slaves were not exempt. The farmers and planters called out, most of whom were over forty years of age, soon began to petition the governor to be allowed to return home and "pitch their crops," arguing forcibly that unless crops were planted, corn would not be raised in sufficient quantity to feed either the army or the people. But with Grant pounding at Vicksburg and Federal cavalry raiding

into northern and even central Mississippi, Pettus refused to disband the militia. Some were furloughed,
however, and so many deserted that the companies
were not half full at the end of March. For some reason the men were not paid, although there was said to
be money in the state treasury, and this added to their
discontent. Apparently there was fault on both sides.
But the militia of Mississippi seems never to have become an effective force for the defense of the state.
In October there was the remarkable spectacle of a
company of state troops deserting in a body to be mustered into the Confederate service! Was it because
life was richer and fuller in the Confederate army? If
so, that may explain why higher militia officers re-
peatedly reported mutinous conduct on the part of
their men. Not only the men themselves but their
families at home were complaining of the withdrawal
of the able-bodied men from the fields or from supervision of the Negroes, who were idling away their
time or running off to the Federals or piloting raiding
parties of Yankees to the plantations. Some locally
raised cavalry companies were accused of robbing on
their own account instead of protecting the helpless
people from the raids of the enemy. Throughout the
Confederacy many of the militia were getting out of
hand. Certainly they were scorned by the veteran soldiers in the army. Listen to the contemptuous description of both "exempts" and militia by the brave and
blunt General Daniel H. Hill as he congratulated his

own soldiers in North Carolina for their courage, patience, and good conduct:

How much better is it thus to deserve the thanks of the country by your courage and patience, than to skulk at home as the cowardly exempts do. Some of these poor dogs have hired substitutes, as though money could pay the service every man owes to his country. Others claim to own twenty negroes, and with justice might claim to be masters of an infinite amount of cowardice. . . . Others are warlike militia officers, and their regiments cannot dispense with such models of military skill and valor. And such noble regiments they have! Three field officers, four staff officers, ten captains, thirty lieutenants and one private with a misery in his bowels! . . .

If the condition of many people, who were at least safe within the Confederate lines, was hard and getting worse, the lot of those whose homes were in sections overrun by the Federals, or between the 'two hostile lines, can be described only as pitiful and perilous. They were likely to be robbed by wandering bands of foragers of clothing, livestock, and food, and unless some humane officer were present, to be maltreated in person. All too often the Federal officers were indifferent to the fate of these unfortunate people who were usually helpless old men, women, and children. If they escaped with their lives, they were left with nothing to eat except what they could pick up in the woods or fields. Many a dark tragedy oc-

[56]

curred there whose story will never be known. What wonder that hundreds of them took the oath of allegiance in order to procure food for hungry and helpless members of their families!

Partly out of the desperate condition of these people who were left near the enemy lines and partly, of course, out of the desire for private advantage, there arose one of the most difficult problems with which the state and Confederate authorities had to deal— illegal and clandestine trade with the enemy. The greater part of this trade centered upon exchanging cotton for supplies. When the war began the southern people believed that their cotton would prove a decisive economic and political factor in their favor. Even the blockade would work to their advantage because it would produce a scarcity of this necessary staple in the world markets and force European nations to intervene in order to obtain it. It became a primary policy of the government to prevent the North from obtaining southern cotton. Trade with the enemy in any way was naturally forbidden. The Congress had passed an act in May, 1861, prohibiting, under severe penalties, the exportation of cotton or cotton yarn from the Confederate States except through one of its seaports or through Mexico. On the other hand, the United States government was as anxious to procure cotton for the northern factories and for export as the Confederacy was to prevent it. Notwithstanding Lincoln's proclamation of August 16, 1861, prohibiting trade or intercourse with the inhabitants of the insurrectionary states, as soon as the Federal armies reached the borders of the cotton country the President granted licenses to traders who swarmed behind the Union armies. The southern states also passed laws to prohibit trading with the enemy and empowered their governors to order the destruction of cotton that was likely to fall into northern hands. The Confederate Congress authorized the destruction of such property by an act of March 17, 1862. When the Federals first came into the cotton region of the Mississippi in the spring of 1862, many patriotic planters in Arkansas, Louisiana, western Tennessee, and northern Mississippi burned their own cotton when they could not get it away. When others hesitated or refused to destroy their property, state and Confederate officers undertook the work of destruction themselves. Nevertheless, some cotton owners managed to save their cotton, either by the neglect of the officials, or by means of influence, or by hiding it in the woods. In this interior region there was no market for cotton within the Confederacy as far as legitimate exportation was concerned, because the only outlets were too far away. But the licensed northern traders were near at hand, offering higher prices than cotton had brought in sixty years, and offering, too, at relatively low prices, a great variety of articles practically unobtainable in the Confederacy. Many of the planters had become regretful of their previous

[58]

haste in destroying their earlier crop and, when the new if shorter yield of 1862 was picked, saw no advantage in raising cotton only to have it burned. Some had managed to hide and save a portion of the great crop of 1861. The temptation to exchange their cotton for supplies proved irresistible to many hitherto loyal planters as well as to thousands of small farmers and hard-pressed wives of poor soldiers who had been able to grow a few bales. By the fall of 1862 a brisk, if somewhat furtive, trade had sprung up, not only in the sections held by the Federals, but also across the military lines. The Union army officers, when they did not actually encourage the business or secretly take part in it themselves, were obliged to honor the orders of the Secretary of the Treasury and President Lincoln. So clothing, shoes, salt, furniture, foodstuffs, and a great variety of other articles, as well as Federal greenbacks and some gold, began to flow into the areas occupied by the Union forces and to trickle into the outer fringe of those still held by the Confederates. Undoubtedly, this opportunity to exchange for absolute necessities the cotton which they could not use saved many a family from wretchedness; but it had the effect also of undermining and destroying whatever loyalty to the Confederate cause still lingered among these people, except when the cruelty of Union soldiers aroused a new hatred for the invaders. This is not difficult to understand, for those who profited from this clandestine trade understood that, since it was only the Confederate laws that they were violating, punishment was to be expected only from Confederate authority. They would, therefore, do nothing to increase that authority or to restore it. They also realized that the relief or profits which the trade brought them would come to an end if the Federal armies should be driven away. This, at least, seems to have been the reaction of most of them— and this in a section where less than two years before the secession movement had been supported overwhelmingly. It is no wonder that thoughtful and loyal Confederates looked upon this illicit and growing trade with increasing apprehension.

And yet, some of the state governments and the Confederacy itself out of their desperate need for articles which could not be procured within their borders, either openly or by connivance, engaged in this trade. And when the people knew that responsible public officials were trading cotton across the lines for supplies, although probably for the benefit of the soldiers, they could not be convinced that it was wholly wrong to have a part in it themselves. What the responsible officials did will be discussed later; it is sufficient here to point out that this trade marks the beginning of one phase of the administrative demoralization which is so apparent in the last stages of the Confederacy's existence.

Having surveyed briefly the increasingly difficult conditions among the people behind the military lines of the Confederacy, as they revealed themselves by the spring of 1863—conditions which were to become more trying with every passing month—let us turn now to see what was done by the state and Confederate governments to solve these perplexing problems. We shall see that the measures taken, generally with the approval and, in truth, at the demand of the people, involved an unprecedented extension of political authority and control which not only would never have been tolerated before the war but which ran counter to the whole political philosophy of the southern people. Of course, these were held to be emergency measures, applicable only to an unusual and desperate situation; but they show something of the willingness to dispense with principles and practices no longer workable and to adopt other methods. And these Southerners, it should be remembered, were fundamentally a conservative people. The attempt to make the measures work also shows how difficult it is to set up a new and extensive administrative system that will function efficiently in an emergency.

Of all the difficult problems that demanded quick solution at the hands of the public authorities, that of alleviating the privations of the poor seemed the most urgent. Hungry people cannot wait indefinitely. It was necessary to make better provision for the wives, children, and other dependents of the soldiers in the ranks, not only as a matter of justice and humanity but also as an imperative matter of policy, if their men were to stay in the fighting line. During the first months of the war, when there was hope that the struggle would be short, such relief measures as were adopted usually devolved upon the county authorities the duty of raising and administering funds; but these measures proved inadequate by the end of 1862. In some counties civil administration had been demoralized by the approach or raids of the Federal armies; in others where the poor were very numerous the burden was more than those counties alone could bear; while in others still, in the interior richer planting counties, the burden was relatively light. In the winter of 1862–1863, therefore, there was a marked change in the character of the new relief legislation. The legislatures of Mississippi and North Carolina each appropriated $500,000 from the state treasury for general relief of indigent families of soldiers, either the money itself or provisions purchased with the money being distributed among the counties according to the number of destitute families therein. North Carolina made an additional appropriation of $1,-000,000 in February, 1863, to be distributed according to the white population as shown by the census of 1860. Georgia's legislature appropriated $2,500,000 for direct relief in money, $500,000 for the purchase of salt, and $100,000 for the building of factories to make cotton and wool cards. All these appropriations, except the last, were to be distributed by county officials. Louisiana adopted a systematic pension system, providing for the payment of $10 monthly to wives or widows of soldiers in state or Confederate service, the same amount to dependent parents, and $5 each to children and dependent younger brothers and sisters of soldiers. The large sum of $5,000,000 was appropriated early in January, 1863, for this purpose. The police jury of each parish was charged with the duty of making lists of those persons in necessitous circumstances and of distributing the money.

In August, 1863, the Alabama legislature appropriated $1,000,000 to be distributed to suffering families of soldiers, and ordered the state comptroller to procure from the county judges estimates of the amounts necessary for the support of the families in their respective counties and to report at the next session. At that session, in December, 1863, the legislature granted $3,000,000 to be distributed, $1,000,-000 at a time, in January, May, and October, 1864. The families of substitutes were to be included, as also were those of deceased or incapacitated soldiers. Georgia, always one of the most generous in the matter of relief, in November ordered the state quartermaster general to purchase 97,500 bushels of corn and ship it for distribution in sixteen counties of the mountain section where an early frost in September had killed the crop before it matured. In December, 1863, the Georgia legislature, among other heavy ap-

[63]

propriations for indirect relief, set aside $6,000,000 for distribution among the widows, orphans, and other indigent dependents of soldiers.

Virginia, either because of the conservative character of its legislative membership or because its normal production of grain had maintained a better food supply than in the cotton states, had done little for direct relief until the fall of 1863. In October, however, perhaps because of the September frost, the county courts and the incorporated towns were authorized to borrow as much as $10,000 for each 1,000 of white inhabitants and to purchase needed articles for distribution and sale to their citizens. A few days later the Virginia general assembly required the county and corporation courts to have lists made of all the soldiers and sailors enlisted from their counties or towns, with like lists of all their families, widows, minor children, and other dependents and to make suitable and just allowances for their support, the expenditures to be charged against the counties. Relief was also to be given at state expense to refugees from the regions devastated by the public enemy.

Mississippi, in December, at a time when a large portion of the most fertile counties of the state had been overrun, in a most elaborate law required the county boards of police to make complete lists of enlisted soldiers and their dependents as a basis for a state-wide relief system. A half million dollars was appropriated for distribution in cash and a special tax of 150 per cent on and in addition to the regular state property tax was levied for the same purpose. This tax was to be paid into the state treasury as were other taxes and was to be distributed in accordance with local needs. In lieu of this property tax, the county boards could levy a tax in kind, that is, one which should be paid in corn, bacon, and other provisions and supplies, or any taxpayer could pay the special tax in this manner, the supplies thus raised and collected to be distributed in the same manner as the money tax. As an evidence of the difficulties expected, the boards of police were authorized to impress supplies and provisions when emergencies arose, the prices for impressed goods being fixed by arbitration when they could not otherwise be agreed upon.

In December, 1863, North Carolina appropriated another $1,000,000 in state treasury notes (now more valuable than Confederate currency) for soldiers' families. South Carolina in the same month levied a tax in kind of 2 per cent to be paid by the producer on all rice, corn, and wheat grown, on all tolls of grain mills, and a similar tax in kind, but at 5 per cent, on the production of all manufactures in the state, including cotton yarns, leather, and salt. The assessment of this tax was to be based upon the assessment made by the collector of the Confederate tax in kind (under the Confederate law of April 24, 1863). The distribution of the receipts was to be made by the state authorities, as was also an appropriation of $500,000 in cash. In Texas, where conditions were generally better than in the other states, the legislature had first left relief to the counties, but began in 1863 to make appropriations from the state treasury and to give to the state officials greater control over distribution of funds and supplies by local officers.

As prices rose still higher, as the difficulties of transportation increased and the privations of larger groups of the people grew worse in the dark days of 1864, the legislatures adopted more far-reaching measures for relief. In March of that year the Virginia general assembly authorized Governor William Smith to set up a state agency in Richmond to purchase and sell to the people at the lowest possible price raw cotton, cotton and wool cards, yarns, and cloth. The governor was empowered to make requisitions upon all cotton factories in the state for yarn or cloth, according to their capacity, and any factory refusing to comply with the requisition was to be fined $5,000 for each such offense.

In August the legislature of Mississippi made an additional appropriation of $1,000,000 for relief and empowered county commissioners, who were charged with the local administration of the act, to impress provisions, including the surplus crops of those planters who had been allowed exemption from military service in the Confederate army in return for turning over to the army a specified amount of agricultural produce. If the county commissioners could not procure enough supplies in their own county they were authorized to go into another county and, upon proof of need, require its sheriff to impress provisions, as well as teams, wagons, and drivers, for their use. In March of 1865 Mississippi imposed a tax in kind of 2 per cent on the gross amount of all corn, wheat, and bacon to be produced that year, on all tolls from grain mills, on the gross profits from the manufacture of leather, yarns, cotton and woolen fabrics, of iron foundries, sawmills, machine shops, of all mechanics, and of dealers in grains, provisions, salt, tobacco, horses, mules, hogs, and cattle. The tax in kind was to be based upon the returns to the Confederate assessors. In December, 1864, South Carolina renewed its tax in kind but equalized the assessment at 3 per cent on both agricultural and manufactured products.

There were certain manifest and significant trends in this later relief legislation. One was the shift from local to state control. It was in the interest of greater efficiency and a more equal distribution of the burden. Another was the change from a money tax to a tax in kind and from the distribution of cash to the distribution of provisions and other supplies. The collapse of the currency made necessary these direct donations of food and clothing. This was a slower and clumsier method of relief, however, because of the time and trouble involved in collecting quantities of bacon, corn, and clothing, storing them in places of deposit, and measuring them out to the needy recipients. Finally, the resort to requisitions and impressments, as in Virginia and Mississippi, reveals the demoralization of the markets and the desperation of the people.

But the state governments did not confine their activities in behalf of their distressed people to the distribution of money, clothing, and food. One of their major efforts was to procure and distribute a supply of salt which, as has been said before, was not merely an essential ingredient of food for human beings and livestock, but was at that time an absolute necessity in curing and preserving meat, especially pork. Without salt, there could be no bacon; in fact, without it people could not slaughter their hogs or beeves, for the meat would spoil. We have already seen how the scarcity of salt, after the clamping down of the blockade, had sent the price shooting skyward; how there was a strong disposition of dealers to buy all they could and hold it for higher prices and profits; how in the first winter there had been a universal outburst of rage as the cost of this hitherto cheap article had risen beyond the means of the mass of farmers and planters; and how some of the governors had begun to impress salt in the hands of dealers, while others had placed an embargo on salt and provisions. Whether because of these impressments and embargoes or solely because of a growing scarcity, the price continued to rise, and public officials, in response to a universal demand, began to look about for a better source of supply. For there was danger that a continued salt famine might, through reduction of the meat supply, wreck the defensive power of both the armies and the people.

The first effort of the state governments, in response to popular demand, was to encourage private parties or corporations to engage in the manufacture of salt. Some private concerns had already undertaken to enter this business, but their success was limited. Furthermore, there was a general suspicion that these concerns would themselves become profiteers unless held in check. Nearly every state east of the Mississippi had made appropriations during 1861 and 1862 for the encouragement of various manufactures and most of them had specifically included salt. The governors of Alabama, Georgia, South Carolina, and North Carolina, with the consent of their legislatures, had entered into contracts with different companies for the production of salt. In all these cases the state gave assistance to the saltmakers and either received a share of the salt made, or contracted for a certain number of bushels at a fixed price, or had prior rights of purchase. But these arrangements did not yield nearly as much as was needed, and the state officials found it very difficult to enforce the agreements with the contractors. The need still being very great, the governors and legislatures began to plan to erect state salt works for the benefit of the people at large.

In the states east of the Mississippi there proved to be three important sources of salt supply. The great-

est was the enormous deposit at the little town of Saltville, on the line of Smyth and Washington counties,
in southwestern Virginia. The second in importance
was on the lower Tombigbee River in southwestern
Alabama, chiefly in Clarke County. The third was the
seacoast or, more particularly, the salt marshes which
lay along the coasts of the Atlantic and the Gulf. West
of the Mississippi were some important salines in
northern Louisiana and northeastern and southwestern Texas; and early in 1862 a great deposit was discovered at Avery's Island near New Iberia in southwestern Louisiana. Of course small salines were found
in other places in different parts of the South, but the
chief reliance for a domestic supply was on these
sources. Since many of the deposits were privately
owned and operated, it became necessary for the states
either to lease ground for their works or to impress
the private works. As the best deposits in Clarke
County, Alabama, were on state lands, the state authorities leased grounds both to private operators and
to state contractors and erected state works for itself.
North Carolina set up its own works on the coast near
Wilmington under the direction of Jonathan Worth.
South Carolina and Florida made similar use of their
coasts. Mississippi obtained some salt from the new
mine at Avery's Island until Federal gunboats on the
Mississippi River cut off that supply. In the spring of
1863 the island fell into the hands of the Federal
army. Virginia, after threatening to seize the works

at Saltville, then monopolized by the firm of Stuart, Buchanan, and Company, was able to make a favorable contract with that company by which the cost of salt to Virginia citizens was greatly reduced. The resources of Saltville were so great that other states sent agents there and entered into contracts or leased wells for themselves. The state of Texas reserved for its own use a salt lake on public lands in the Rio Grande Valley. Every state that could do so entered directly into the business of making salt for distribution to its own people. In many instances the governor also imported salt on state account for sale or donation to the needy.

The initial scarcity of manufactured articles of nearly all sorts had early in the war turned the attention of legislators to the necessity of encouraging additional factories. Many new companies received charters, but few of them seem to have gone into actual operation because of the difficulty of obtaining machinery when the foundries were all busy with work for the Confederate government. The factories already in existence were soon busy with contracts for the army or the state militia and were able to place but little of their production on the public markets. As prices rose, however, they soon found more profit in selling to dealers than to the state or Confederate governments, although the latter at first allowed them a profit of 75 per cent above the cost of production. As it became more difficult to persuade the manufacturers to enter into new contracts with the government, the conscription enrolling officers began to conscript or threaten to conscript the workmen. The first exemption acts had been liberally construed in favor of the factories and an act of Congress of October 8, 1862, had permitted machinery for making cloth and shoes to be admitted duty free. During 1863 and especially after the more stringent Conscription Act of 1864, the Confederate quartermaster general began forcing the cotton and wool factories to contract a larger share of their output to the government on pain of taking away their operatives. Before the end of the war a large portion of the production of the cotton factories was being monopolized by the government for the use of the armies.

Certain of the states had, in the meantime, entered into contracts with the factories within their own borders either for articles needed by their militia or, as in North Carolina, for shoes and clothing for their troops in the Confederate service. Later they demanded cloth for their destitute families. Occasionally there was a sharp conflict with the Confederate officials over rival claims to the output of some factory. Because of the difficulty of procuring machinery and skilled operatives, and also because of the problems of management, the states seldom attempted to set up factories themselves. But there were exceptions. Texas established a very successful cloth factory in the state penitentiary, and sold or donated the cloth to its people; and it established a state foundry at Austin for making cannon and munitions, which it finally turned to the manufacture of plows and of spinning jennies for making cotton yarns. Georgia attempted to set up a state factory for making cotton and wool cards for the people of that state. Other states also had foundries for making or repairing arms. After the energetic Henry W. Allen became governor of Louisiana in January, 1864, he exported cotton to Mexico, brought back stocks of medicines, cotton cards, and other essential supplies, erected a state store, a state dispensary for medicines, a cotton card factory, two small cotton cloth factories, purchased a one-fourth interest in an iron furnace in eastern Texas and with the iron obtained from it erected a foundry for making cooking utensils and agricultural implements. Unfortunately, some of these establishments had not long been in operation when the general collapse came in the spring of 1865. The Confederate government, through the quartermaster's and ordnance bureaus, built shops, foundries, armories, and powder mills. But for the needs of the people, who must be looked after by the states, contracts with manufacturers and importations were usually relied upon. These measures did but little to keep prices within reach of the middle-class families. One is forced to the conclusion, however, that only circumstances, not theoretical principles, prevented either the states or the Confederacy from entering into the business of manufacturing on an extensive scale.

One subject that deserves more consideration than time will permit is the expansion and changes in the state tax systems. Because of their heavy bonded debts created in 1861 the states began to increase the tax levies in 1862. Almost immediately it became necessary to remit or postpone tax collections in those counties of Tennessee, Arkansas, Mississippi, Louisiana, and Virginia that had been overrun by the enemy, and as the Federals penetrated farther into the country other large sections became delinquent. As the poorer regions fell into greater poverty, the returns of the tax collectors became shorter, so that the burden was borne by an ever smaller proportion of the people. The depreciation of the currency and high prices received for the products of the farm and plantation, on the other hand, made payment easier for those who could raise and market crops until the adoption of the tax in kind both by the Confederate government and certain of the states. Mississippi in January, 1863, temporarily defaulted in the payment of interest in specie on certain bonds issued by the Convention of 1861, because, as declared by a legislative resolution, specie was no longer obtainable, a large portion of the state was overrun by the public enemy, the rest was menaced, and "no nation, to meet its admitted obligation, is bound upon principles of public and national law to ruin or destroy its people." There was a strong tendency in many states to place a larger and larger share of the tax burden upon those groups which seemed best able to bear them. The legislature of Georgia, for instance, in a resolution of December 14, 1863, declared that the *ad valorem* system should be combined with the *net income* system and immediately passed a law imposing a graduated tax on incomes. Several other states, like Virginia and Mississippi, imposed a profits tax which was very nearly an income tax, but these laws may have been directed against speculators as a class rather than in furtherance of a new principle.

The continuous rise in the cost of living, especially in the towns and in remote districts where crops had failed, was becoming a matter of increasingly grave danger. On February 24, 1864, the market reports of the Richmond *Examiner* quoted the best grades of flour at $225 to $250 per barrel, corn at $28 to $30 a bushel, meal at $30 to $35 per barrel, new bacon at $6 to $6.50 per pound, apples at $90 to $110 per barrel, brown sugar at $11 to $12 per pound, sorghum molasses at $40 per gallon, and onions at $35 per bushel. Potatoes were cheap, only $10 to $14 per bushel. In June of 1864 the same paper in quoting prices listed at Columbia, South Carolina, asserted that they were not more than one fifth of the Richmond prices for the same articles. The early legislation against monopolies and extortion had become a dead letter and apparently no effort was made to revive it. The restrictions on the planting of cotton and tobacco, however, were renewed and continued. Whether it was because of the legislation or because of the poor market for cotton and the increased demand for foodstuffs, the cotton crop had fallen off steadily. The yield of 1861 had been estimated at 4,500,000 bales, that for 1862 at a little more than 1,500,000, that of 1863 at less than 500,000, and that of 1864 fell below 300,000 bales. The prohibition laws against the distillation of grains were re-enacted and extended to every other article which the ingenuity of man had been able to convert at the stills. If we may judge from what is preserved in the official and private correspondence of the period, public sentiment strongly upheld these restrictive laws which were so opposed to the individualistic traditions and habits of the people.

But there was one expression of government authority to which the mass of the people never became reconciled, unless we except those who benefited directly, as hungry soldiers in the army and their families on relief. This was the practice of impressment. So loud were the complaints that Congress, on March 26, 1863, passed "An Act to Regulate Impressments." This law, however, did not prohibit impressment; on the contrary, it legalized it, but it did attempt to do away with certain abuses which had become too common. Under this law, when the purchasing officer and

[76]

the owner could not agree upon the price of the article in question they were to choose local arbitrators, and if their decision was acceptable to the officer he was to give the owner a certificate showing his authority, the military command to which he belonged, a description of the article, and the price. In case the price fixed by the arbitrators was unsatisfactory to the officer, he could appeal to the state board of impressment commissioners. This board, as provided by the law, was to consist of two citizens of the state, one appointed by the President and one by the governor. Their chief duty was to determine upon and publish, at least every two months, a schedule of prices to be effective throughout the state, for all articles needed by the government. When the two commissioners could not agree they were to select a third who was to act as umpire. The price schedules were to be the guide for all purchasing officers within that state. While the act provided for compensation of the owners for all articles impressed, it carefully refrained from providing for the payment of open market prices. Consequently, impressment prices were consistently much lower than those paid by private purchasers and never satisfied those whose goods were taken under the law. From the point of view of the owners, the only improvements made by the law were, first, the requirement of local arbitration, which amounted to little if the state board overruled the local arbitrators; and second, the care taken to make sure the impressing officer was a genuine official and not a mere fraudulent impersonator.

As we have already seen, the state legislatures also authorized impressments by the governor or his duly appointed agents when certain articles were needed for the public defense or for the relief of the poor. Some of these acts were even more sweeping than that of the Confederacy; but the most interesting of them provided for the impressment of slaves, or slave labor, for work on military fortifications. These last were induced by a section in the Confederate law which authorized the impressment of slave labor according to the method prescribed by the state law, or in the absence of such a state law, under such regulations as the Secretary of War should prescribe. Those states which had neglected to provide for the impressment of slaves hastened to give authority to the governor to draw out some proportion of the slaves when called upon either by the President or by the general commanding the department. There is ground for suspecting that legislators who were not themselves slaveowners, or who represented constituencies where there were few slaves, were glad to make this use of the property of the large planters.

It had become evident before the end of 1861 that both the Confederate government and the people must rely upon purchases abroad to satisfy certain of their imperative needs. The Confederate authorities and some businessmen acted at once, but the states did not enter the business until later. Texas seems to have been the first state to undertake officially the exporting and importing business. A state Military Board, organized in January, 1862, and composed of Governor Francis R. Lubbock and two other state officers, soon undertook to purchase cotton with state bonds and to export it to Matamoros on the border of Mexico where it would be exchanged for military supplies. The board encountered so many difficulties, because of the competition of private traders, the long distances to be traversed by their caravans—for there were no railroads within three hundred miles of the border—the trouble in procuring wagons, teams, and drivers, the inefficiency or peculations of some of its agents, the robbery of its trains by bandits who infested that border region, the frequent interference of Confederate officials, and the unstable political and military situation along the Rio Grande, that it accomplished but little. After more than two years of its operations it could show but 5,736 bales of cotton purchased and less than that number sold. A new board, constituted in April, 1864, with Governor Pendleton Murrah in complete control, seems to have accomplished even less. Its most notable contribution was a long wrangle with General Edmund Kirby-Smith, the commander of the Trans-Mississippi Department, who had set up a Cotton Bureau for the control of the cotton business on the Rio Grande.

Blockade-running along the South Atlantic and Gulf coasts had become a regular and thriving business by the beginning of 1862, and some of the adjacent states had contracted with the runners for the delivery of supplies. In November, 1862, the new governor of North Carolina, Vance, planned to put his state directly into the business. He sent agents to England to purchase supplies for the North Carolina soldiers and to buy a steamer for use as a blockade-runner. The steamer was purchased and, under its new name, the *Advance,* became famous. Later, in 1863, Vance purchased a one-fourth interest in three other vessels which assisted in taking out cotton and bringing in supplies for both soldiers and the people. So successful were Vance's operations that other governors desired to emulate him. Governor Brown of Georgia entered the business for his state early in 1864 by purchasing a half interest in a steamer, and the South Carolina legislature authorized the purchase by the state of a one-fourth interest in the prosperous Importing and Exporting Company of South Carolina, one of several such corporations previously chartered by the legislature. A little later Governor Smith of Virginia also took his state into this business, but without, so far as is known, buying any vessels.

The Confederate government, through its several purchasing bureaus, had been engaged all along in exporting and importing through the blockade under agreements with the shipping companies. But President Davis, like many others, had become greatly concerned over the importations by private persons of large quantities of luxuries—such as silks, liquors, and other things which seemed unnecessary to a people struggling for existence—and at his suggestion Congress passed two acts on February 6, 1864. One prohibited the importation of a long list of luxuries; the other prohibited the exportation of cotton, tobacco, military and naval stores, sugar, molasses, and rice except under such regulations as the President should prescribe, and imposed heavy penalties for the violation of the law. When the regulations of the President appeared, it was discovered that all privately owned vessels were required to carry half of their outgoing and incoming cargoes on Confederate government account. Although state-owned vessels were exempted from the application of the law, the privately owned vessels under contract with them were not. The intrusion of the Confederate government sometimes left the owners of the vessels no cargo space for themselves, whereupon they refused to take any cargo at all. The law, strictly interpreted, therefore interfered directly or indirectly with the freedom of the states to contract for shipments and caused some very sharp controversies. Davis, however, would not recede from his position.

We have now traced a remarkable development of political authority over the ordinary activities of the southern people during their desperate struggle for

independence. It was remarkable because it represented a complete break with their traditions and
their whole political philosophy. It may seem all the
more strange that there was so little popular opposition to some of the most stringent measures. Of
course, it was the feeling that these things were necessary to their own ultimate welfare that caused the
people to accept so much of this governmental control
without complaint. There were, to be sure, some doc-
trinaires who never reconciled themselves to what
was being done; but the mass of the loyal element
complained chiefly because the measures taken were
not more effective. Next we shall look into the administration of some of these laws and try to see why,
in spite of them or because of them, the economic life
of the beleaguered Confederate people weakened and
disintegrated.

III

FAILURE AND DISINTEGRATION

IN THE preceding chapters we have watched the emergence of unexpected, perplexing, and dangerous economic and social problems brought by the war upon the civilian people of the Confederacy; and we have noted the measures taken to meet those difficulties. Upon their solution depended the ability of the people, from whom the armies drew their strength, to continue to support the war. It needs no elaborate argument to show that the courage of the men in the ranks and the skill of their officers would be nullified by the collapse of the economic resources and the morale of the people behind the battle front, for these were citizen-soldiers and fundamentally the men with Lee and Joseph E. Johnston and the people at home were one. We now turn to trace the results of the measures taken to free the people from their economic entanglements, to give better organization to their remaining resources in the hope of making them more effective, to restore strength and confidence, and to save the general morale.

Certainly the outlook was discouraging during the

winter of 1863–1864. The military situation was frankly bad. Vicksburg had been lost and now Chattanooga was lost; powerful forces of the enemy were gathering to thrust at the very heart of the Confederacy. Lee had failed at Gettysburg and was again on the defensive in Virginia, his effective strength sadly depleted, his men in rags and half-fed. Behind the lines, despite every effort to relieve their distress, thousands of families were nearer starvation and nakedness than ever before. Desertions had become alarming and large sections of the mountain areas had been taken over by combinations of deserters, Unionists, and predatory bands who terrorized the country round about and defied the constituted authorities. With few exceptions, the railways were all but broken down. Feeble engines dragged little trains of eight to ten cars over worn-out tracks an average distance of less than a hundred miles per day. The Confederate currency had continued to fall and in January of 1864 was worth only about four cents in gold. Expecting it to collapse entirely, those who could do so refused to take it and not only the people but even government purchasing agents were turning to barter. Quartermasters offered nails, cotton yarns, and cotton cards for corn and bacon. Congress, in desperation, passed a Funding Act in February with the design of calling in the redundant old currency and replacing it with a smaller amount of a new issue; but, although this stopped further depreciation for some three months,

[84]

the funding provision failed to accomplish its purpose and, partly because it involved partial repudiation by the government, the treasury notes of the government fell again toward zero.

If I were asked what was the greatest single weakness of the Confederacy, I should say, without much hesitation, that it was in this matter of finances. The resort to irredeemable paper money and to excessive issues of such currency was fatal, for it weakened not only the purchasing power of the government but also destroyed economic security among the people. In fact, there seems to be nothing vital that escaped its baneful influence. But if you then ask me how, under the conditions which had existed in April, 1861, the Confederate government could have avoided this pitfall, I can only reply that I do not know. With the small amount of gold and silver coin available in the South and with the initial necessity of using a large portion of that supply in making necessary foreign purchases, how was it possible for this debtor section to accumulate a supply of gold large enough for its needs, or to keep treasury notes at par? The United States government, with infinitely greater financial resources, could not do it! Of course, some contemporary critics of Memminger, the unhappy Confederate Secretary of the Treasury, asserted that the government should have bought up or seized all the cotton, placed it in warehouses, and used it as a basis of credit abroad for the purchase of a navy with which to break up Lincoln's blockade, and thereby open the way for southern exports to go out and for gold and supplies to flow in. Others insisted that the Confederate government should have based its note issues on a straight cotton loan, or that it should have taken over the crop of cotton and other exportable products, paying the planters for all these things with the treasury notes and then made the cotton, tobacco, and other crops, in the absence of gold, the foundation or backing for its currency. But a brief analysis of these proposals will show that they were impracticable. In the first place, at that early stage of the war an attempt of the government to seize the cotton would have been regarded as a flagrant usurpation of unconstitutional authority. To seek to buy it all in the open market would have resulted in a great inflation of the price. But if this could have been done, how was the government to get the cotton to Europe when there were no vessels in southern ports to carry it through the blockade? And if a large European loan could have been negotiated on the basis of the cotton, whether exported or held within the country, how could the Confederate government, in the face of the threatening attitude of the United States, have prevailed upon Great Britain or France to sell armed and manned warships to the unrecognized Confederacy? The proponents of the plan airily dismissed all these questions, but the difficulties were real for those who had the responsibility for adopting a definite policy. As to basing the currency upon cotton purchased from the planters, would that have left the government, hard pressed as it was for cash for military expenditures, a sufficient supply of sound money in the treasury? With the cotton locked up within the country and virtually unsalable, would not the treasury have been obliged to issue more currency? Could it have brought the original issue back into its vaults by an initial system of high taxes? No other modern nation has been able to finance successfully a long war by taxation alone. There is no need to go further, for if the issue of an unsupported currency could not be avoided in the beginning there was no place where it could be stopped later. Depreciation and enhancing costs called for more treasury notes which resulted in further depreciation and higher prices; and thus the vicious downward spiral, once entered upon, could not be stopped until utter ruin had resulted. The one point that is insisted upon is that, under the conditions existing at the beginning, the resort to paper currency was unavoidable. And there was no turning back when once that course was taken.

It is very unlikely that the early rise of the price level was caused wholly by the currency policy, for the rise was very uneven and actual physical scarcity accounted for the rapid increase in the cost of such articles as salt, coffee, wool, leather, tea, and medicines. The first efforts to check the rising costs, through embargoes, seizures, and acts prohibiting monopolies and speculation, failed, as they were doubtless bound to fail. They caused hoarding and greater scarcity. The only final remedy was increased production or the use of suitable substitutes. In the winter of 1861–1862, by general popular agreement, a program for a greater production of foodstuffs was undertaken. It worked well enough to have some effect, and before the end of another year popular clamor caused several state governments to enforce the plan by imposing restrictions upon the planting of cotton. During 1863 every state except Louisiana and Texas—in which no such necessity existed—laid restrictions upon the planting of cotton or tobacco. It worked imperfectly, for we find complaints in some districts that many persons were disregarding the law and we hear practically nothing of the enforcement of penalties against them. On the other hand, the astonishing decline in the production of cotton—from 4,500,000 bales in 1861 to less than 300,000 bales in 1864—indicates that there could have been no general disregard of the law with respect to that staple. We have no statistics on the production of tobacco, but there is ample evidence that this crop also was reduced heavily. Although there were failures in both corn and wheat crops in 1862, the yield of 1863, except in the mountain sections and in the areas overrun by the Federals, seems to have been a large one. Especially in those plantation sections far enough in the interior to be safe from Federal attack and where slave labor was still undisturbed, the grain crops were larger than ever before.

Again there are no reliable statistics, but if we may accept the statements of many observers, enough grain was raised, especially corn, to feed all the armies, the people, and the livestock. The difficulty was in making an equitable distribution of the grain.

Working out a system of equitable distribution required disentangling a network of interrelated problems. To what extent, in law or equity, were those who had plenty responsible for those who had little or nothing? If it be granted that, in the interests of both humanity and sound public policy, they must accept responsibility, how was the distribution of relief to be administered? Should foodstuffs and other commodities for the suffering be purchased in the open market at exorbitant prices or should they be impressed? Should the local political units be responsible for the relief of their own poor or should the state as a whole assume the obligation? How was prompt transportation of bulky commodities to be obtained over the weak and overloaded railroads and in rural communities where wagons and teams had become so scarce that they hired at $30 or more per day?

We have seen that the earlier relief measures which placed all responsibility upon the county officials were soon changed to a state-wide system in which funds were appropriated from the state treasury and control centralized under the governor. The county officials were then used as local administrators of relief and were to be held to strict accountability for their use of

[89]

the funds. Then, as the value of the currency fell, the tax in kind replaced the money relief tax, and food, salt, and clothing were distributed instead of cash. The resort to impressment of supplies for those on relief reveals something like desperation during the closing months of the war. The distribution of supplies directly was attended with extraordinary difficulties because of the extra labor and time required and the scarcity of transportation. In those sections where disorder was prevalent—and there was much disorder during the final winter—the ordinary difficulties of collecting, storing, and disbursing were greatly aggravated.

The recipients of relief were not always satisfied. Some of them charged favoritism on the part of distributing officers, others insisted that certain of these officials were appropriating for themselves and speculating in the articles intended for the widows and orphans of soldiers, and still others claimed that deserving persons were overlooked. If we may assume that many of these complaints were inspired by nothing more than suspicion, jealousy, or a mean desire to make trouble, we must admit that, if they were all untrue, there was a singular purity and unselfishness displayed by the accused. At any rate, however generous and patriotic the motives of those who were responsible for the relief measures, the administration of those measures did not entirely allay dissatisfaction. They may have prevented the growth of discontent and disloyalty in many communities, but if we may judge by the attitude of those in whom hostility to the Confederacy was conspicuously displayed as early as 1863, they did not win back much support to the Confederate cause. On the contrary, desertion and disloyalty continued to spread.

The defensive strength of the armies was kept below normal not only by desertions but also by various devices for evading conscription. Some malingerers obtained habeas corpus writs from state courts, while others, with the aid of clever lawyers, got from those courts favorable construction of the exemption provisions. One lawyer in Lexington, Virginia, recorded sixty-eight cases handled by him before the local court in February, 1864, with fees in some cases running as high as $500. He wrote to a brother lawyer that there "is a good time coming for our fraternity." But the most prolific source of exemptions was the plea of ill-health backed by the certificate of a physician. The number of these evasions irritated the men who were doing hard service in the field and worried Confederate officials and all others who wished to see the armies recruited to their fullest possible strength. The Richmond *Dispatch* early in February, 1864, satirized the shirkers in a biting editorial:

Things which were once regarded as evils have now become objects of esteem. The various "ills that flesh is heir to" are no longer considered ills. Rheumatism, which was once dreaded as a torturing fiend, has become as popular as a beautiful coquet, tormenting and yet enchanting her spellbound victims. There's "a tear in the eye and a smile on the lip" of each of its successful votaries. Gout is also much sought after; but in these hard times few families can get above rheumatism. Gout would cost as much money as a substitute, but "rheumatism" can be had without the cost of a dollar. Where fuel is so scarce and wet weather so abundant, there is no one too poor to afford rheumatism. . . .

Old age, once at an awful discount, has now become an object of universal respect. Men who once shuddered at the idea of becoming old, now look upon a grey beard with religious veneration. They who so long dreaded the downhill of life would now cheerfully barter their vigorous prime for a grey beard, a weak back, and pipe-stem legs. No school boys ever slid down a snowy declivity as they would slide down the winter side of life, if they could. Alas for them! Every dog must have his day. These envied old fellows have spent many a bitter hour in relaxing their hold upon the joys of youth, and brooding over the ashes to which their bright expectations have turned. They have felt the pangs of waning influence, the contumely of being hustled from the various walks of active life by younger and more vigorous men. It must be some compensation for their miseries that old age has at last become honorable, that there are so many ingenious youths who prefer its crutches to the warrior's sword, and who would rather drink gruel and sleep with its legs in flannels than lap up human blood or be smothered in a bed of laurels.

But the thing that caused the most widespread dissatisfaction was the practice of impressment. The act of Congress in March, 1863, to regulate the manner of impressing necessities for the use of the government failed to do away with the evils which had developed earlier. This was mainly because of two things. One was the emergency needs of certain commanders in the field, especially outside of Virginia (for General Lee rarely permitted impressment within the limits of his immediate command). In such cases free rein was given to quartermasters and commissaries who impressed right and left with little consideration for the needs of the unfortunate owners. The other was the disorganization of the supply departments and the inability of the heads at Richmond to inform themselves fully of what their subordinates in distant parts were doing. This left lazy or unscrupulous officers free of control and enabled them to disregard the safeguards of the law with impunity. Backed by a squad of soldiers they took what they wanted without permitting a local board of arbitration to adjudicate the price, as was required by the law, and either failed to pay for the articles seized or gave no certificates or false ones. In the last case, the officer was usually covering up his own private peculations. It is no wonder that the title of "quartermaster" became, in many sections, a term of derision and hatred. To add to the confusion, wandering companies or regiments of Confederate cavalry, in constant need of corn for their horses as well as food for themselves and out of reach of depots of supplies, began to live off the country in real freebooting fashion and became as much dreaded as the Yankees. General Joseph Wheeler's cavalry in particular had a bad reputation in this respect. In still other cases, bands of robbers and marauders, when they did not steal and murder outright, frequently amused themselves by assuming the character and authority of impressing officers and doing their robbery under pretended legal forms. Their unfortunate victims could seldom distinguish between the legal and the illegal and hated all alike. If we may accept the statements of reliable Confederate officials in all parts of the country—and there is no reason why we should not accept them—the conduct of both the impressment officers and wandering bands of undisciplined cavalry and mounted militia was responsible for the growth of disloyalty and the spread of Unionism in many communities that had been staunchly loyal only a year earlier. In such cases the paralysis of the arm of the government is very apparent.

I have referred several times to the difficulties of transportation throughout the Confederacy. This was another major problem and perhaps ranked next to finances in its deleterious consequences. There is not time to go fully into the subject, but it should be pointed out again that the southern railroads in 1860 were relatively new, and that they were all short lines, controlled, with few exceptions, by local companies with limited financial resources, and practically unregulated by law. Designed for local tranportation— for carrying crops down to the river towns or seaport —they were stocked with a small number of engines and cars and few of them had shops where they could make needed repairs. Nearly all of them had obtained their engines and cars from northern machine shops, except a few that had bought from the Tredegar Iron Works in Richmond. The rails in common use were mostly narrow strips of wrought iron. The T-rail had only recently come into use and had been placed on very few southern roadbeds. The gauges, that is, the widths between the rails, varied from three to six feet, so that cars on roads of different gauges could not be transferred from one line to another. One southern journalist counted eleven different gauges on the southern roads. Under the stress of traffic the light engines and cars began to break down and the rails to wear out. Replacement was difficult and little help could be had from the government which had its hands full of other problems. Throughout the war the condition of the roads deteriorated, partly from inability to replace or to repair efficiently worn-out rolling stock and rails, and partly because military officials sometimes impressed engines and cars and took them

[95]

off into other states where they were likely to be lost or abandoned, if not captured. It is easy to find instances of roads which had been fairly well equipped at the beginning of the war, left by 1864 with two or three broken-down engines and less than one fourth of their freight cars. Some roads were actually abandoned when their rails were taken up and used on other and more vital lines. Other roads had all their spare rails impressed by the Navy Department for covering ironclads or Confederate gunboats. At terminal points, where a difference of gauge forced the unloading of cars and the reloading of freight on another line, goods frequently piled up in warehouses because the second road was unable to provide cars or engines. Delays ensued that were extremely irritating to both government officials and businessmen. There are numerous instances where foodstuffs, such as grains, remained so long in these places that they rotted under leaky roofs or were eaten by weevils before they could be taken on. It was a common complaint, backed by reliable evidence, that abundant stores of corn and bacon and stocks of clothing stayed in railroad warehouses while the men in the armies at the front and poor people on relief, for whom they were intended, were half-clothed and half-starved. Another charge against the railroad companies was that they frequently gave preference in shipments to speculators' goods because they received therefrom higher rates and prompter pay; and this seems not

unreasonable because both Confederate and state officials forced such close bargains for government traffic
that the roads made little or no profit from that class
of business. The Confederate authorities forced all
roads to give priority to Confederate shipments, and
some states, as Virginia, demanded priority for their
own freight over all except Confederate business.
When the military authorities were confronted by delays on a road they were quite likely to impress the
road and all its rolling stock and to stop private shipments, so that not merely the merchant but whole communities in need of salt or corn that had been paid for
could not get them shipped. Quite naturally, all these
impediments and hindrances caused bitter comments
and loud complaints, and often a governor felt called
upon to protest to the military authorities. Be it said
to the credit of the latter that they usually did what
they could to forward relief supplies. Another evidence of dissatisfaction is the frequency with which
legislatures ordered an investigation of some railroad
company.

But, as has been indicated, the railroads were not
altogether to blame for their poor service, for they
were confronted with difficulties beyond their power
to overcome. Gradually they fell more and more
under the control of the War Department which
forced them to do its bidding or else run the risk of
both impressment and the conscription of employees.
But their condition became worse and worse, thus

making the task of feeding the army and serving the needs of the people more hopeless of fulfillment. When the war ended they were all but useless.

But the broken-down railroads are only a part of the picture. By far the greater part of local transportation had to be carried on by wagons, carts, and teams. There were a few wagon shops in the South in 1860, but most of these vehicles, so essential to local needs, were imported from northern shops. As the average period of usefulness of a farm wagon was only a few years, those already in use could not be expected to last through the four years of war. Under the hard service they broke down rapidly, for farmers were often forced to take them long distances over execrable roads—nearly all wagon roads were bad in those days—in order to procure salt or other supplies, especially as the service of the railroads was curtailed. The army needed large numbers of wagons and bought so many early in the war that the supply left for civilian use was depleted. As the supply declined, many small private wagon shops sprang up, but difficulties beset the operators in the scarcity of seasoned woods for wheel spokes and felloes, or iron for axles, tires, and bolts, and in the loss of workers by conscription. The government also set up its own shops, but they were never able to keep pace with the loss and waste of the armies. Moreover, the impressment of wagons and teams during the last two years of the war became so common that owners were afraid to

[98]

venture out on the roads, especially within the sphere of active military operations. The only wagons that were safe from the impressing quartermasters were those that were really unfit for use. The same difficulties applied to teams. Horses and mules had become so scarce by the end of 1863 that the armies were poorly provided, especially for cavalry and artillery use. While the principle was recognized that the agricultural interests of the country and the production of food required that farms and plantations should be left sufficient teams for the cultivation of crops, this principle did not deter impressing officers from taking horses and mules that were needed both on the farms and in the army. When the Federals raided Confederate territory they took particular care to take away all horses and mules. In many parts of the Lower South oxen had been used to a great extent, especially among the poorer farmers; but these, too, declined in number as they were either impressed for use as teams or for beef. In consequence of all these things, wagons and teams had practically disappeared from many communities as early as the spring of 1864. How much this almost universal breakdown of transportation contributed to the growing paralysis of the economic activities of both the people and the government may easily be imagined.

The industrial weakness of the Old South, its paucity of manufactures, is so well known that it needs little comment. With more than a fourth of the total

[99]

population of the Union, in 1860, counting the Negroes, it produced only from a twelfth to a tenth of the total manufactured articles which had become essential to economic and social well-being, and of some things much less than that. For more than twenty years thoughtful men had urged that Southerners turn their attention more to manufacturing and a "mixed industry" and less to planting staples. Some progress had been made before secession, but for many reasons, which need not be recited now, southern people were still dependent upon northern and foreign mills, mines, shops, and foundries for fabricated articles. When the war and the blockade closed down, the factories which had been built became hives of industry; and everywhere men, eager for the profits they saw in the mounting demand for scores of manufactured articles, endeavored to build new plants that would "relieve us forever from paying toll to Yankee capital and mechanics." Legislatures chartered many a manufacturing company in every year of the war, but very few actually went into operation. Either the initial capital was lacking, or the necessary machinery could not be obtained, or skilled workmen were unavailable. In some cases we are led to suspect that the companies so readily formed were merely for promotion purposes, or were based upon the slender prospects of fat contracts from the government which never materialized.

But there were many small factories, mills, and

shops in tangible form, actually turning out yarns and cloth, bar iron and finished iron wares, shoes and other leather goods, lumber and various types of woodwork. With a demand for their products far greater than they could supply, it would seem that the owners of these enterprises, if anybody could, would reap a rich harvest. And many of them did, for a while. Most of the early contracts for army supplies made with them by the quartermaster general and by governors allowed them very high profits: frequently these contracts were on a "cost plus" basis, stipulating a profit of not more than 75 per cent on the total cost of production. But since the manufacturers had no incentive to keep costs down—rather it was to their interest to increase them in order to swell the 75 per cent profit—prices went up so rapidly that army officials complained and state authorities became indignant. The result was that new contracts began to be forced upon them stipulating fixed prices or lower profits for large quantities of their products. When actual costs to the manufacturer began to rise rapidly —for materials, for labor (which advanced but little, however), and for new machinery, they received little sympathy from the purchasing officials. And when many of them refused to sell their excess products to the people for less than the highest market price, they were denounced far and wide as "stony-hearted speculators."

Then more troubles came. Worn-out machinery

could seldom be replaced except through the blockade, for the few foundries in the Confederacy that could make it were too busy manufacturing arms and other articles for the government. The machinery must be purchased in England, paid for by the exportation of cotton, and then must run the blockade. Whole sets must be bought, for it was next to impossible to find parts that would fit the rest of the machinery. If, as sometimes happened, the cargo was lost, the whole procedure had to be repeated at great expense of money and time. The operators were always having trouble with railroads which could not, after 1863, bring raw materials needed except with the consent of the quartermasters who controlled transportation or of impressment officers and conscript hunters. Even though their workmen might once be exempted, there was no assurance that they would not be called out later. After the new Conscription Act of February 17, 1864, which abolished previous exemptions and authorized the Secretary of War to detail men for certain necessary civil services, the factory owners were entirely at the mercy of some government bureau. They could not obtain details of men unless they made contracts for supplying the government, and their men were detailed for only sixty days at a time. Not infrequently they were compelled to turn over to the Confederate purchasing officers their entire production, except what was necessary to exchange for raw materials or for food for their hands.

Beginning in the fall of 1863, when Confederate treasury notes had become useless for purchasing supplies, the factories were compelled to set up commissaries for their employees and to barter cloth, yarn, nails, leather, or whatever they had for corn, meal, bacon, and other foodstuffs. By 1864 they were paying their hands in material things because currency was worthless. Even then, many of them were being paid by the government in currency. Thus the manufacturing industries suffered in the end with the farmers and planters and all the rest. They had been brought under a control that was nonetheless effective for being indirect; but it was less the control than the collapse of the currency that ruined them.

Viewed at this distance, the industrial weakness of the South was one of the decisive factors in its defeat, not merely because of the appalling scarcity of so many essential articles—even of such common things as axes, spades, hammers, nails, pins, needles, plows, hoes, horseshoes, steam engines, wool and cotton clothing, shoes, harness, wagons, and scores of other commonplace necessities—but also because the colonial economy which had been so characteristic of southern business before the war had left the country without sufficient fluid capital or coin to sustain the currency. Foreign purchases, as well as paper treasury notes, had drained out the specie. The absence of a "mixed industry" is merely a part of the whole hopeless situation. The danger came to be thoroughly

understood soon after the war began, and efforts were
made to fill the gap when it was too late. "It is the
northern mechanic," said one southerner, "who is de-
feating us."

You will recall that state-owned or state-controlled
salt works were set up in southern Alabama, along the
coasts, and at Saltville in southwestern Virginia.
These enterprises had a measure of success, but they
struggled under many difficulties from the beginning.
The works on the coast were frequently interfered
with by military officers who impressed teams and
boats, conscripted the workers, and sometimes closed
down the works on the suspicion that the men were
communicating with the enemy's blockading squad-
rons. Raiding parties from blockading ships at times
captured the works, drove off the working force,
burned the buildings, and broke the furnaces and vats.
There was always a shortage of transportation. At
Saltville there were squabbles between rival state
agencies over the use of water rights, over the scanty
fuel supply, and over prior rights of transportation on
the weak little railroad that connected Saltville with
the Virginia and Tennessee Railway a few miles away.
This road could not carry away a fifth of the salt that
could be made. The state agents chafed at the delays,
and the people who were impatiently waiting for salt
with which to cure their meats complained loudly.
Even after the salt was transferred to the Virginia
and Tennessee there was much difficulty in getting it

by roundabout routes into Georgia, Mississippi, or the Carolinas, for the line through Tennessee was blocked by the Federals after the fall of 1863 and that down the eastern seaboard was choked with other traffic. The Confederate government held priority on all shipments; the military at times interfered by seizing all the trains; and finally, in December, 1864, Federal raiders captured Saltville and demolished the works. But in spite of all hindrances these works were able to supply the people with at least a portion of the salt needed and, in Virginia, to reduce its cost. In that state salt was the only important article that was cheaper in 1864 than in 1862.

One other example of failure to establish real control, rigorous as were the measures provided, was in the trade across military lines. The beginning of this commerce, chiefly in cotton, has already been described. As time went on and the scarcity of raw cotton in the world market became more alarming, the price had risen rapidly toward one dollar per pound. Its price within the Confederacy varied according to locality, but was always relatively low because little of it could be utilized locally. Late in 1864 it sold in western Louisiana for twenty cents in Confederate currency, which was less than one cent in gold, when the price in New York was over forty cents in gold. Moreover, the total production had steadily fallen off because of the demand for foodstuffs and because of legal restrictions placed upon its cultivation. In the areas near the lines of the enemy, as in Mississippi and Louisiana, the opportunities for exportation or sale to northern buyers would doubtless have resulted in more extensive planting had it not been for the disturbance and complete loss of slave labor in some cases and the certainty in others that Confederate officials would impress or buy under threat of impressment most of the crop as soon as it could be gathered.

All through these exposed regions there was great confusion not only among the hapless people but also in administrative circles as well. The laws could not be enforced except by military authority; but the military was itself disorganized, its discipline breaking down except in the veteran units in the larger armies. State officials were virtually helpless in the face of the disorder. Small bands of patrols, some of them detached cavalry units, others "home guards," moved about arresting disloyal persons and cotton runners, and, if reports may be relied upon, living off the country by impressments that amounted to little less than open robbery. Whether they did more good than harm is an open question. But certainly they did not put an end to illegal trading.

Throughout 1864 the outward smuggling of cotton went on wherever opportunity offered and the opportunity was found near the Federal lines. In some communities poor families banded together, and women and children, with a few old men as companions for protection, loaded cotton on a small caravan of decrepit wagons with such horses or mules as had been hidden from marauders and impressment officers, and crept slowly along byroads, past Confederate patrols, and into the towns held by the Federals on the Mississippi. They had to pay the cotton tax and sometimes buy a license, but so eager were the Federal buyers to get cotton that they gave encouragement to all smugglers. Selling it at a good price, these people bought supplies and returned in the same way to their homes. These were the poor whose necessities had driven them to smuggling. But many wealthy planters showed no scruple in conveying large quantities of cotton to the river bank at designated points where boats met them, took the cotton, and paid in gold and greenbacks. In some of the river towns certain citizens engaged regularly in the traffic by taking oaths of loyalty and getting permits from the Federal officers to bring out cotton from behind the Confederate lines. Many of the most successful smugglers and traders in a local way were women. They became adepts at evading such regulations as either Union or Confederate authorities laid down, either by misrepresentation of the facts or by "greasing the palms" of the officers. How much bribery of this sort went on will never be known, but the opportunities for peculation by officers of both armies were such that few men in a period of such general demoralization could have resisted the temptation altogether.

We find evidence that southern men, no longer connected with the army, made their way to New Orleans and got permission from the Union authorities there to bring in cotton and ship it out. This much was easy, for it was not against the policy of the government at Washington. It was not so easy to get permission to ship supplies back to points within the Confederate lines, which was against the declared Federal policy, but they obtained permits for that also, usually under the thin pretense that these goods were for the supply and relief of the suffering civilian population. But when the shipments consisted of army blankets and shoes, tent cloth, and other quartermaster's stores, and these things passed out from the Federal lines with the permission of Federal officers, one is justified in suspecting that somebody's hands had been greased. For it must be remembered that, as far as peculation was concerned, there was fully as much demoralization among Federal as Confederate officers. It is probable that there was even more, for those who had access to the outer markets had far greater opportunity and temptation to dally with this sordid business than those who, like the Confederate officers, were cut off from the huge profits possible in New Orleans. The amounts at stake may be illustrated by a single instance. A trader from New Orleans entered into a contract with the chief Confederate quartermaster in the Trans-Mississippi Department in December, 1863, which permitted the trader to buy 2,000 bales of cotton in Arkansas with Confederate money, ship the cotton to New Orleans, bring in supplies for the Confederate army, and receive in return for those supplies 13,200 bales of cotton which he was to ship in turn to New Orleans. By this transaction he would, on an initial capital of $40,000 in United States currency, make a net profit, after all ordinary expenses were paid, of about $5,000,000 in greenbacks. And it was claimed that this was one of the most favorable contracts for the Confederacy that had been made!

There were some strange things happening, strange at any rate to those who are accustomed to believe that hostile armies never willingly furnished each other with supplies. In January, 1864, a citizen of New Orleans made arrangements with General Richard Taylor, whose headquarters were then in Alexandria, to bring boats up the Red River, load them with cotton belonging to the Confederate army, take the cotton to New Orleans, and bring back supplies for the Confederates. Since the transaction was manifestly to the advantage of the Confederates in that they were to obtain badly needed supplies, no blame can attach to General Taylor nor *perhaps* to the trader, who had formerly been in the Confederate service and professed to be actuated by patriotic motives; but what is one to think of the Union army officers if they permitted their enemy to be thus provided for? As a matter of fact, the transaction was a violation of the law of the Confederate Congress, but the exigencies of the army had made that law a dead letter. Jefferson Davis himself had on occasion given permission for cotton to be sent out through the enemy's line, but he always stipulated that it was *not* to be shipped to a *northern* port—a promise that the trader was very willing to make—and doubtless comforted himself with the reflection that it was a way of running the blockade with Federal help.

Shortly after these transactions took place, General Nathaniel P. Banks, commanding at New Orleans, proposed to President Lincoln that, as it had proved impossible to stop the trade in cotton from behind the Confederate lines, it be permitted to send out cotton through New Orleans and to have a personal credit of eighteen cents per pound deposited in favor of the trader in the hands of the government, the rest of the proceeds of the cotton to be placed in the United States treasury. Banks argued that "where your treasure is, there will your heart be also," and that once these Confederate officers had large sums to their credit with the United States government, they would cease fighting, go over to the Union side, and by wholesale withdrawal leave the Confederate army completely demoralized and unwilling to fight longer. He stated that a recent shipment of 15,000 bales to the mouth of the Red River had been made with that arrangement in view. How the plan appealed to Lincoln is not disclosed.

But the trade went on. Confederate army officers, unable to procure supplies for their men with worthless Confederate currency, in desperation arranged to exchange cotton, now worth more than forty cents a pound in gold in New York, for food, clothing, shoes, or whatever they most needed. And they had the aid of the administration at Washington in one instance that we know of. In the dark winter of 1864–1865, when General Lee's half-starved and depleted army was holding the trenches around Petersburg and Richmond, it was being fed with bacon that was brought from New York City to the coast of North Carolina, whence it was sent inland and exchanged for cotton. The cotton went to New York and the bacon was sent up to Lee's army at Petersburg where Grant was trying to cut off Lee's supplies! The crowning touch of irony to this true story is that the exchange was carried on by the special permission of President Lincoln and was stopped by a peremptory order from General Grant when he discovered what was happening.

When common people saw this official trade going on in violation of the law, while they were held liable to punishment for doing the same thing, is it any wonder that they did not understand the fine distinction between a violation of the law for the benefit of the army and their own violation of the same law for the benefit of their families? Is it any wonder that they were grumbling and suspicious of the officials who sent out cotton but would not let them do the same thing? Is it surprising that those who managed, nevertheless, by stealth or by corrupt connivance, to profit from the commerce with the Yankee traders, came to look upon the presence of Federal troops as at least no worse than that of Confederates? If we may judge by the evidence, nothing proved more demoralizing to the loyalty of the people in these border areas than this tempting but illicit traffic.

Let us now survey briefly the situation behind the lines late in 1864 and endeavor to sum up what had been attempted and what accomplished by way of solution of the major problems affecting the civilian population. It is unnecessary to say very much about conditions in those last dark days of that desperate struggle, for we have already seen something of the confusion, disorder, suffering, discontent, and evidences of disloyalty which spread from one end to the other of the devastated and fire-encircled southern country. To those loyal and courageous men who looked the situation over calmly and saw it clearly, the prospects must have seemed dismal indeed. With large sections of their original territory lost beyond power of recovery, cut in two along the Mississippi, and being cut through again as General William T. Sherman's hordes swept like a resistless avalanche downward from the smoldering ruins of Atlanta toward Savannah and the sea; with one point after another on the coasts falling into Federal hands, and with the only southern army of which much could now be hoped straining every ounce of its failing strength to hold the lines around Richmond and Petersburg while its ragged, shoeless soldiers shivered in the cold and lived on less than half rations; with the remnants of the armies of the West and Southwest demoralized and disintegrating, what could they hope for? But this was not the worst. The country upon which these remaining forces depended for support was no longer in condition to give much support. Food there was in plenty in some sections, but it could not be transported in sufficient quantity to feed the soldiers. The internal administration was broken or breaking everywhere except in a few regions where able and energetic governors and army officials had maintained a little order in the general chaos. The fierce loyalty and enduring courage of a large portion of the people were nullified by the apathy and indifference, and too often the open hostility, of other groups who were still beyond the immediate reach of the public enemy. But everywhere there was deadly weariness of the war—weariness of bloodshed and hardship, of insecurity, of the evident hopelessness of the apparently endless struggle. The morale of the people was disintegrating rapidly as the whole social order moved toward collapse.

As we look backward over what had happened it becomes very clear that the southern people had not been able to solve the internal problems which the war had raised. *Could* they have solved them if they had been able to anticipate them and if they had adopted other measures? That is a hard question, but my present conviction is that only a series of miracles would have made it possible. If they had been opposed to a power of no more than equal strength, they might have won; but they were constantly forced to exert their utmost strength, and every mistake was costly. The strain on their resources was terrific and the government had no choice but to sacrifice one interest to another, the one which seemed of less immediate concern to that which seemed greater. To most of the higher army officers and to Davis himself, keeping the army at full strength in order to hold the enemy at bay naturally seemed the most important thing, but this is not to say that they were indifferent to or neglected other considerations. For instance, it seems clear enough that both Congress and the President made a sincere effort to work out a system of selective service for the army that would do the least damage possible to the economic and social structure upon which the armies must rest; but they were without precedent or experience or any accurate means of analyzing the needs of the civilian population. And they had failed to take into account the class jealousies aroused by certain exemptions such as the twenty-Negro clause provided in the conscription acts. When they tried later to remedy these errors, if they were errors, the damage was already done and could not be corrected. The Confederate government moved steadily, if rather slowly in some matters, toward more and more control over the ordinary activities of the people, but it was the desperate situation that forced it in this direction. Of course this development aroused opposition but there was criticism on the other hand because the government did not move rapidly enough.

The state governments also wrestled with these internal difficulties and greatly extended their control over matters formerly regarded as outside the functions of government. These things they did not only in the interest of their own people but also in behalf of the common cause and to assist the efforts of the Confederate government. Much has been said about the controversies over state rights within the Confederacy—and of course there were such controversies—but it needs to be pointed out that the state governments, including the individual governors, exerted themselves far more in loyally assisting the general government than in thwarting it. And in these policies the state governments were sustained by the mass of the people.

But let us look back at these internal problems upon whose solution depended the maintenance of the southern struggle for political independence. One, perhaps the most important, was that of finances. Here there was complete failure and the wonder is that the government was able to hold up for so long after its credit and currency had utterly collapsed. The war had to be financed on credit; but there was no basis for such an amount of credit except the staple crops, and they could not be utilized to any great extent because of the blockade and the lack of a navy strong enough to break that blockade. Granted that there were initial mistakes on the part of the states as well as of the Confederate government in resorting to treasury notes and bonds, these measures were exactly those which any people with small monetary resources and hopeful of early peace were likely to adopt. And what else could they have done? We have seen how many of the later difficulties followed as a consequence of disordered finances.

All efforts to check price inflation proved futile. Some of them, such as embargoes and seizures of speculators' goods, were bound to fail. There could have been no remedy for inflated prices but a sound currency, ample production, and an adequate system of transportation. The limitation of cotton and tobacco planting, though not perfectly administered, seems to have had good effects. Enough food was produced, but it could not be distributed where it was needed. The relief measures adopted by the states unquestionably did much good, but they never worked with entire satisfaction because of the loss of purchasing power in the currency, the disturbances incident to wartime, the difficulties in getting food, salt, and clothing to those in need, and the forced resort to the clumsy method of bartering for supplies. The consequence was plenty in some communities and near starvation in others. Nevertheless, all things considered, it is hard to see how the authorities could have done more.

But impressments, one result of currency troubles, were extremely unpopular and it is a question whether they did as much good as harm. They did not check the ruinous rise of prices and they did in far too many cases deprive plantations and farms, factories and shops, of the means of greater production and they helped to break down the railroad service. Worse still, they outraged the feelings of hitherto loyal people, leaving with them a bitter sense of wanton injustice. Of course, this was not the intention of the authors of the impressment policy, but the execution of the law was left in the hands of men who, in the nature of their work, could not be closely supervised, who were concerned only in getting supplies in the easiest way, who had no local responsibility, and who, more and more, became demoralized by opportunities for peculation. No other one thing, not even conscription, caused so much discontent and produced so much resentment toward the Confederacy.

The transportation problem, also a vital matter to both the people and the armies, was never properly diagnosed. The inherent difficulties were enormous, but had there been foresight and intelligent planning at the beginning, the railroads could have stood up better under the strain. After Quartermaster General Alexander R. Lawton had virtually taken over control of the roads at the end of 1863, he and some of his subordinates did what was possible to rehabilitate the lines, but it was then too late. The railroad officials themselves, representing a multitude of small lines, were never able to co-ordinate their policies and services, and when the army and state officials tried to remedy the faults of train service by force, their interference too often resulted merely in disrupting it. There were no men trained in railway economics or in operation on a large scale. It was all a sort of rule-of-thumb business. Probably railway development had not then reached the stage for centralized control, but the lack of any such control, except such as the quartermaster general exercised, prevented a solution of the problem. As to local transportation by wagons and teams, I have already explained that the inability to make wagons as fast as they broke down, the wear and tear on the horse and mule supply in army service, and the impressment of a large portion of those that were needed in agriculture and in hauling crops left this essential service paralyzed.

Trade with the outer world went through the same transition from unregulated private enterprise, which fostered speculation, to state trade activities, and finally to Confederate control during the last year. The Confederate law of February 6, 1864, by which the President was empowered to establish regulations for all export and import trade, was less an attempt to extend the power of the government than it was to put an end to waste of resources on useless importations and to provide supplies for the army that could not otherwise be had. It extended the President's power and not only aroused the opposition of thoroughly loyal governors by interfering with their own activities in behalf of their people, but also gave opportunity to the critics of Davis to charge him with dictatorial ambitions. Strangely enough, it had been urged early in the war that the government do this very thing, but it was not done until the last year. The plan did not work satisfactorily because the regulations imposed did not fit the situation of all regions. It did not work well in Texas, for instance, where the commanding general of the Trans-Mississippi Department had established a Cotton Bureau on different principles, which, because of the peculiar situation there, were really preferable to the President's regulations. But because the law prescribed uniformity, Davis forced the dissolution of General Kirby-Smith's Cotton Bureau. And on the Atlantic and Gulf coasts the blockade was tightening down so that the great days of blockade-running were past. Confederate control came too late to accomplish much for the government.

As to the illegal trade with the enemy, we have already seen how futile were the efforts to stop it; but it is interesting to see to what lengths the efforts went —arrest and imprisonment of the traders, at times; the confiscation of the cotton, at times. But the stakes were so high, and the methods of control were so inefficient, that the traffic was checked but little, except where the military was strong enough to seize all the cotton itself and do its own trading on army account.

Summing it all up, it can be said that the southern people and their governments failed, with a few exceptions, to conserve, develop, and efficiently administer their resources; but it must be said that these were gigantic tasks, intricate, complex, and baffling. That they did not succeed better is not surprising when we remember the simplicity of southern economic and political organization before secession. There was not time, while a powerful and determined enemy was crashing at the gate, to reorganize their whole system and, without previous experience, develop a far-reaching and studied policy, create a complex administration, and train administrators. Problems had to be met as they arose; and unexpected problems arose with bewildering rapidity, demanding instant solution. All in all, it is not surprising that they could not be solved, or that, in the end, the collapse was complete.

In these lectures I have been concerned primarily with what seem to me to have been certain fundamental problems of the Confederate people and, necessarily, with their failure to solve those problems. It is on the whole, I fear, a depressing story. But I do not wish to end croaking the word "failure." I prefer to end on a different note and in simple justice to those people to pay a brief if inadequate tribute to their courage and steadfast loyalty to their failing cause under trials and hardships of which we can have but a faint conception. Of course, not all of them deserve such an encomium, for there were some among them who were weak in spirit and selfish in conduct. But I am thinking of those ragged, hungry men who fought on after they knew their cause was hopeless, and of those women at home who cheerfully endured privations and subdued their fears while they struggled against every sort of adversity to provide for their children and other dependents while their men were at the front. And while I have had much to say about some forms of selfishness and sordidness, because the desperate conditions of the war brought out the worst in some men and helped to make the problems of the rest more difficult, I feel that I should be somehow unfeeling if I did not here at the last pay tribute also to the unpretending generosity of thousands of the more fortunate to their less fortunate neighbors. The evidences of that kindly generosity will run like threads of gold through the woven tapestry of any adequate account of the history of the people of the Southern Confederacy. Perhaps the Lost Cause was doomed from the beginning of the war, but its gallant and courageous people upheld it until their whole economic and social order disintegrated and collapsed about them. And they went on to the tragic end, aware of what was impending, without faltering. For that they will live, with honor, throughout history.

A BIBLIOGRAPHY OF THE WRITINGS OF
CHARLES W. RAMSDELL

I. Books Written

Reconstruction in Texas. 324 pp. *Studies in History, Economics and Public Law,* edited by the Faculty of Political Science of Columbia University, Vol. XXXVI, No. 1 (New York: Columbia University, Longmans, Green and Company, 1910).

A School History of Texas (with Eugene C. Barker and Charles S. Potts). 384 pp. (Chicago: Row, Peterson and Company, 1912).

Behind the Lines in the Southern Confederacy. The Walter Lynwood Fleming Lectures in Southern History at Louisiana State University, 1937. 136 pp. (Baton Rouge: Louisiana State University Press, 1943).

II. Books Edited

The History of Bell County, by George W. Tyler. xxiii, 425 pp. (San Antonio: Naylor Company, 1936).

Laws and Joint Resolutions of the Last Session of the Confederate Congress (November 7, 1864– March 18, 1865) Together with the Secret Acts of *Previous Congresses.* xxvii, 183 pp. (Durham: Duke University Press, 1941).

III. PUBLISHED ARTICLES AND ESSAYS

"Martin McHenry Kenney," in the *Quarterly of the Texas State Historical Association,* X (1906–1907), 341–42.

"Texas from the Fall of the Confederacy to the Beginning of Reconstruction," *ibid.,* XI (1907–1908), 199–219.

"Presidential Reconstruction in Texas," *ibid.,* 277–317.

"Texas in the Confederacy, 1861–1865," in *The South in the Building of the Nation,* 13 vols. (Richmond: Southern Historical Publication Society, 1909–1913), III, 402–17.

"Texas in the New Nation, 1865–1909," *ibid.,* 417–47.

"The Last Hope of the Confederacy—John Tyler to the Governor and Authorities of Texas," in the *Quarterly of the Texas State Historical Association,* XIV (1910–1911), 129–45.

"The Frontier and Secession," in *Studies in Southern History and Politics,* inscribed to William Archibald Dunning (New York: Columbia University Press, 1914), 61–79.

"Internal Improvement Projects in Texas in the Fifties," in the *Proceedings of the Mississippi Valley Historical Association,* IX (1915–1918), 99–109.

"The Confederate Government and the Railroads," in the *American Historical Review*, XXII (1916–1917), 794–810.

"Historical Election Ballots," in the *Southwestern Historical Quarterly*, XXIII (1919–1920), 308–309.

"The Control of Manufacturing by the Confederate Government," in the *Mississippi Valley Historical Review*, VIII (1921–1922), 231–49.

"The Texas State Military Board, 1862–1865," in the *Southwestern Historical Quarterly*, XXVII (1923–1924), 253–75.

"The Preservation of Texas History," in the *North Carolina Historical Review*, VI (1929), 1–16.

"The Natural Limits of Slavery Expansion," in the *Mississippi Valley Historical Review*, XVI (1929–1930), 151–71. Reprinted in the *Southwestern Historical Quarterly*, XXXIII (1929–1930), 91–111.

"Early Chapters in the History of the (Texas) Interscholastic League," in the *Interscholastic Leaguer*, XIV (1930), No. 3.

"General Robert E. Lee's Horse Supply, 1862–1865," in the *American Historical Review*, XXXV (1929–1930), 758–77.

"The Southern Heritage," in William T. Couch (ed.), *Culture in the South* (Chapel Hill: University of North Carolina Press, 1934), 1–23.

"Some Problems Involved in Writing the History of the Confederacy," in the *Journal of Southern History*, II (1936), 133–47.

"One Hundred Years of Progress in Texas, 1836–1936," a preface to *Texas Centennial Edition, Encyclopaedia Britannica* (New York: Encyclopaedia Britannica Company, 1936).

"The Changing Interpretation of the Civil War," in the *Journal of Southern History*, III (1937), 3–27.

"Lincoln and Fort Sumter," *ibid.*, 259–88.

"Carl Sandburg's Lincoln," in the *Southern Review*, VI (1940–1941), 439–53.

IV. Unpublished Papers

"The United States Indian Policy in Texas and the Public Lands," read before the Mississippi Valley Historical Association, Madison, Wisconsin, April 15, 1921.

"The Problem of Public Morale in the Confederacy," read before the joint session of the American Historical Association and the Mississippi Valley Historical Association, Richmond, Virginia, December, 1924.

"Barker as a Historian" (manuscript in the University of Texas Library, 1926).

"How Slavery Came to Texas," read before the East Texas Historical Association, Huntsville, March 1, 1927.

"Materials for Research in the Agricultural History of the Confederacy," read before the joint session of the American Historical Association and the Agricultural Historical Society, Chapel Hill, North Carolina, December 31, 1929.

"Was There a Reasonable Probability That the Election of Lincoln Meant an Attack upon the Institution of Slavery Within the States?" read before the Mississippi Valley Historical Association, Chattanooga, Tennessee, April 25, 1930.

V. CONTRIBUTIONS TO BIOGRAPHICAL AND HISTORICAL DICTIONARIES

A. *Dictionary of American Biography,* 20 vols. and index (New York: Charles Scribner's Sons, 1928–1937), edited by Allen Johnson and Dumas Malone.

Baker, Daniel, I, 517.
Baker, William Mumford, I, 527.
Baylor, Robert Emmet Bledsoe, II, 77–78.
Bell, Peter Hansborough, II, 160–61.
Burleson, Edward, III, 286–87.
Burleson, Rufus Clarence, III, 287–88.
Burnet, David Gouverneur, III, 292–94.
Coke, Richard, IV, 278–79.
Culberson, Charles Allen, IV, 585–86.
Culberson, David Browning, IV, 586–87.
Gorgas, Josiah, VII, 428–30.
Lubbock, Francis Richard, XI, 480–81.
Memminger, Christopher Gustavus, XII, 527–28.
Myers, Abraham Charles, XIII, 375–76.

Neighbors, Robert Simpson, XIII, 407–408.
B. *Dictionary of American History,* 5 vols. and index
(New York: Charles Scribner's Sons, 1940),
edited by James Truslow Adams and R. V. Cole-
man.
Army, Confederate, I, 109–10.
Confederate States of America, The, II,
9–13.

VI. BOOK REVIEWS

A. *American Historical Review*
John Bach McMaster, *A History of the People
of the United States During Lincoln's Ad-
ministration* (New York: D. Appleton and
Company, 1927), XXXIII (1927–1928),
156–58.
John Gibbon, *Personal Recollections of the Civil
War* (New York: G. P. Putnam's Sons,
1928), XXXIV (1928–1929), 367–68.
J. Frank Dobie, *A Vaquero of the Brush Country*
(Dallas: Southwest Press, 1929), XXXV
(1929–1930), 679–80.
Ella Lonn, *Salt as a Factor in the Confederacy*
(New York: Walter Neale, 1933), XXXIX
(1933–1934), 753–54.
James Truslow Adams, *America's Tragedy* (New
York: Charles Scribner's Sons, 1934), XL
(1934–1935), 529–31.
B. *American Political Science Review*

Jesse T. Carpenter, *The South as a Conscious Minority, 1789–1861: A Study in Political Thought* (New York: New York University Press, 1930), XXV (1931), 466–68.

Francis Butler Simkins and Robert Hilliard Woody, *South Carolina During Reconstruction* (Chapel Hill: University of North Carolina Press, 1932), XXVI (1932), 757.

C. *Historical Outlook* [1]

James Ford Rhodes, *History of the United States from Hayes to McKinley, 1877–1896* (New York: Macmillan Company, 1919), XI (1920), 204.

D. *History Teacher's Magazine*

Winfred Trexler Root and Herman Vandenburg Ames, *Syllabus of American Colonial History, from the Beginning of Colonial Expansion to the Formation of the Federal Union* (New York: Longmans, Green and Company, 1912), V (1914), 64.

John Bach McMaster, *A History of the People of the United States, from the Revolution to the Civil War*, Vol. VIII, 1853–1861 (New York: D. Appleton and Company, 1913), V (1914), 97.

John W. Burgess, *The Administration of President Hayes* (New York: Charles Scribner's Sons, 1916), VIII (1917), 279–80.

E. *Journal of Southern History*

[1] A continuation of the *History Teacher's Magazine.*

Douglas Southall Freeman, *R. E. Lee: A Biography*, 4 vols. (New York: Charles Scribner's Sons, 1934–1935), I (1935), 230–36.

J. G. Randall, *The Civil War and Reconstruction* (Boston: D. C. Heath and Company, 1937), IV (1938), 532–33.

Carl Russell Fish, *The American Civil War: An Interpretation* (New York: Longmans, Green and Company, 1937), IV (1938), 533–34.

Avery Craven, *The Repressible Conflict, 1830–1861* (University, La.: Louisiana State University Press, 1939), V (1939), 553–54.

F. *Mississippi Valley Historical Review*

Haywood J. Pearce, Jr., *Benjamin H. Hill, Secession and Reconstruction* (Chicago: University of Chicago Press, 1928), XVI (1929–1930), 124–25.

Ulrich Bonnell Phillips, *Life and Labor in the Old South* (Boston: Little, Brown and Company, 1929), XVII (1930–1931), 160–63.

William Best Hesseltine, *Civil War Prisons: A Study in War Psychology* (Columbus: Ohio State University Press, 1930), XVII (1930–1931), 480–81.

Eric William Sheppard, *Bedford Forrest, The Confederacy's Greatest Cavalryman* (New York: Dial Press, 1930), XVIII (1931–1932), 95–96.

Robert Selph Henry, *The Story of the Confeder-*

acy (Indianapolis: Bobbs-Merrill Company, 1931), XVIII (1931–1932), 587–88.

Annie Carpenter (Mrs. W. F.) Love, *History of Navarro County* (Dallas: Southwest Press, 1933), XX (1933–1934), 304.

Arthur Charles Cole, *The Irrepressible Conflict, 1850–1865. A History of American Life,* Vol. VII (New York: Macmillan Company, 1934), XXI (1934–1935), 279–81.

George Fort Milton, *The Eve of Conflict: Stephen A. Douglas and the Needless War* (Boston: Houghton Mifflin Company, 1934), XXII (1935–1936), 105–106.

Robert McElroy, *Jefferson Davis: The Unreal and the Real,* 2 vols. (New York: Harper and Brothers, 1937), XXV (1938–1939), 426–28.

G. *Southwestern Political and Social Science Quarterly*

Charles Howard McIlwaine, *The American Revolution: A Constitutional Interpretation* (New York: Macmillan Company, 1923), V (1924–1925), 282–84.

Charles Seymour, *The Intimate Papers of Colonel House Arranged as a Narrative,* Vols. I and II (Boston: Houghton Mifflin Company, 1926), VII (1926–1927), 307–10.

Don C. Seitz, *The Dreadful Decade, Detailing Some Phases in the History of the United States from Reconstruction to Resumption,*

[131]

1869–1879 (Indianapolis: Bobbs-Merrill Company, 1926), VII (1926–1927), 326–27.

James G. Randall, *Constitutional Problems under Lincoln* (New York: D. Appleton and Company, 1926), IX (1928–1929), 357–59.

Albert J. Beveridge, *Abraham Lincoln, 1809–1858*, 2 vols. (Boston: Houghton Mifflin Company, 1928), X (1929–1930), 432–36.

Charles Seymour, *The Intimate Papers of Colonel House Arranged as a Narrative*. Vols. III and IV (Boston: Houghton Mifflin Company, 1928), XI (1930–1931), 96–99.

H. *Southwestern Social Science Quarterly* [2]

Minnie Clare Boyd, *Alabama in the Fifties: A Social Study* (New York: Columbia University Press, 1931), XIII (1932–1933), 87–88.

Edith Gittings Reid, *Woodrow Wilson: The Caricature, the Myth and the Man* (New York: Oxford University Press, 1934), XV (1934–1935), 366–67.

I. *Southwestern Historical Quarterly* [3]

Oliver Morton Dickerson, *American Colonial Government, 1696–1765* (Cleveland: Arthur H. Clark Company, 1912), XVI (1912–1913), 214–17.

Winfred Trexler Root, *The Relations of Pennsyl-*

[2] A continuation of the *Southwestern Political and Social Science Quarterly.*
[3] A continuation of the *Texas Historical Association Quarterly.*

WRITINGS OF CHARLES W. RAMSDELL

vania with the British Government, 1696–1765 (New York: D. Appleton and Company, 1912), XVI (1912–1913), 214–17.

William E. Dodd, *Statesmen of the Old South, or From Radicalism to Conservative Revolt* (New York: Macmillan Company, 1911), XVI (1912–1913), 332–33.

Edward Channing, Albert Bushnell Hart, and Frederick J. Turner, *Guide to the Study and Reading of American History* (Boston: Ginn and Company, 1912), XVI (1912–1913), 334.

Ernest William Winkler (ed.), *Journal of the Secession Convention of Texas, 1861* (Austin: Texas Library and Historical Commission, 1912), XVI (1912–1913), 430–31.

James Albert Woodburn, *The Life of Thaddeus Stevens* (Indianapolis: Bobbs-Merrill Company, 1913), XVII (1913–1914), 93–95.

Jubal Anderson Early, *Lieutenant General Jubal Anderson Early, C. S. A. Autobiographical Sketch and Narrative of the War Between the States* (Philadelphia: J. B. Lippincott Company, 1912), XVII (1913–1914), 95–96.

Hill Publes Wilson, *John Brown, Soldier of Fortune: A Critique* (Lawrence, Kan.: Hill P. Wilson, 1913), XVII (1913–1914), 318–20.

Charles King, *The True Ulysses S. Grant* (Phila-
[133]

delphia: J. B. Lippincott Company, 1914),
XVIII (1914–1915), 420–22.
Paul Leland Haworth, *America in Ferment* (Indianapolis: Bobbs-Merrill Company, 1915),
XIX (1915–1916), 207.
Carl Lotus Becker, *Beginnings of the American People. The Riverside History of the United States,* Vol. I (Boston: Houghton Mifflin Company, 1915), XIX (1915–1916), 313–14.
Frederic L. Paxson, *The New Nation. The Riverside History of the United States,* Vol. IV (Boston: Houghton Mifflin Company, 1915), XIX (1915–1916), 316.
Carter Godwin Woodson, *The Education of the Negro Prior to 1861: A History of the Education of the Colored People of the United States from the Beginning of Slavery to the Civil War* (New York: G. P. Putnam's Sons, 1915), XIX (1915–1916), 440–41.
James Sprunt, *Chronicles of Cape Fear River, 1660–1916* (Raleigh: Edwards and Broughton Printing Company, 1916), XXI (1917–1918), 424–25.
Anson Mills, *My Story* (Washington: Author, 1918), XXII (1918–1919), 200–202.
Archibald Henderson, *The Conquest of the Old Southwest* (New York: Century Company, 1920), XXV (1921–1922), 222–24.
Albert Burton Moore, *Conscription and Conflict in the Confederacy* (New York: Macmillan

Company, 1924), XXIX (1925–1926), 240–43.

John Donald Wade, *Augustus Baldwin Longstreet, A Study of the Development of Culture in the South* (New York: Macmillan Company, 1924), XXIX (1925–1926), 243–44.

Louis Martin Sears, *John Slidell* (Durham: Duke University Press, 1925), XXX (1926–1927), 156–57.

E. Merton Coulter, *William G. Brownlow: Fighting Parson of the Southern Highlands* (Chapel Hill: University of North Carolina Press, 1937), XLII (1938–1939), 153–55.

Louise Biles Hill, *Joseph E. Brown and the Confederacy* (Chapel Hill: University of North Carolina Press, 1939), XLIII (1939–1940), 262–64.

Ella Lonn, *Foreigners in the Confederacy* (Chapel Hill: University of North Carolina Press, 1940), XLIV (1940–1941), 148–50.

Arndt M. Stickles, *Simon Bolivar Buckner: Borderland Knight* (Chapel Hill: University of North Carolina Press, 1940), XLIV (1940–1941), 150–51.

J. Winston Coleman, Jr., *Slavery Times in Kentucky* (Chapel Hill: University of North Carolina Press, 1940), XLIV (1940–1941), 517–19.

J. *Texas Historical Association Quarterly*

John Rose Ficklen, *History of Reconstruction in*

Louisiana (*through 1868*) (Baltimore:
Johns Hopkins Press, 1910), XIV (1910–
1911), 76–78.

J. B. Polley, *Hood's Texas Brigade, Its Marches,
Battles, and Achievements* (New York:
Neale Publishing Company, 1910), XV
(1911–1912), 90–91.

August Santleben, *A Texas Pioneer* (New York:
Neale Publishing Company, 1910), XV
(1911–1912), 91–92.